MEASURING INVESTMENT PERFORMANCE

Calculating and Evaluating Investment Risk and Return

DAVID SPAULDING

McGraw-Hill
New York   Chicago   San Francisco   Washington, D.C.   Auckland   Bogotá
Caracas   Lisbon   London   Madrid   Mexico City   Milan
Montreal   New Delhi   San Juan   Singapore
Sydney   Tokyo   Toronto

Library of Congress Cataloging-in-Publication Data

Spaulding, David,
   Measuring investment performance : calculating and evaluating
investment risk and return / David Spaulding.
       p.   cm.
   ISBN 0-7863-1177-0
   1. Investment analysis.   2. Rate of return   I. Title.
HG 4529.S62   1997
658.15'2—dc21   97-13946
                                                            CIP

McGraw-Hill

A Division of *The McGraw·Hill Companies*

1 2 3 4 5 6 7 8 9 0   DOC/DOC   9 0 2 1 0 9 8 7

ISBN 0-7863-1177-0

The sponsoring editor of this book was Stephen Isaacs, the managing editor was Kevin Thornton, the editing supervisor was John M. Morriss, and the production supervisor was Suzanne W.B. Rapcavage. It was set in Palatino by Inkwell Publishing Services.

Printed and bound by R.R. Donnelley & Sons Company.

McGraw-Hill books are available at special quantity discounts to use as premiums and sales promotions, or for use in corporate training programs. For more information, please write to the Director of Special Sales, McGraw-Hill, 11 West 19th Street, New York, NY 10011. Or contact your local bookstore.

 This book is printed on recycled, acid-free paper containing a minimum of 50% recycled de-inked fiber.

For Betty, Chris, and Doug

CONTENTS

In 1986, I took over systems for a New York City-based investment adviser. My initial role was to get their portfolio accounting system in order. One thing we quickly learned was that the investment performance measurement component wasn't providing accurate results. Erroneous performance information could prove disastrous, since management uses the information to gauge how they're doing, marketing uses it for attracting new business, and clients rely on performance results to see how well their manager is performing. Bad numbers could cause managers to draw improper conclusions and make poor investment decisions, advertising erroneous performance numbers has very serious legal consequences, and clients don't respond particularly well when they learn that the performance numbers they've been getting are less than accurate. Timely and accurate performance information is essential.

Performance measurement was new to me at the time, so I searched for information to help understand the subject better. I quickly found that there was almost nothing available. I obtained a copy of the Bank Administration Institute's standards (which I'll discuss later), but found it somewhat confusing. One of the biggest aids was an article written by Peter Dietz, but it was not as in-depth as I would have liked. I also brought a consultant in to help with the design of our system, to ensure it complied with acceptable methods.

Over the years, I've obtained greater knowledge of performance measurement from various seminars, conferences, workshops, and articles. But I realized there still wasn't a single source that someone could turn to in order to get a solid grounding in this rather complex topic.

To make matters worse, over the past ten years the subject has grown in many ways. New standards have been introduced, performance attribution and risk are more important, and many firms are seeking ways to look at performance beyond the portfolio level (going up to composites or other groupings and down to security, sector,[1] and other levels).

One thing that happened when I began writing this book was that I came to realize how much I didn't know about some of the various aspects of performance measurement. I'm indebted to many experts who have previously written articles and/or made presentations from which I've picked up additional information. These include Robert (Bob) McAllister of DST/Belvedere; Mike Smith of Financial Models; Brian Singer of Brinson Partners; Steve Lerit of Chase Manhattan Bank; James (Jamie) Hollis of Standish, Ayer, and Wood; Neil Riddles of Templeton Global Investors; and Lee Price of RCM Capital. I especially want to thank Bob, Mike, Steve, and Jamie. They generously undertook the task of reading the manuscript and gave me the benefit of their expert criticisms and suggestions.[2]

In addition to the gentlemen noted above, there are several others who need to be acknowledged.

This book's readability and grammar have been enhanced through the very capable and professional editing skills of Susan Ritchey of McGraw-Hill.

Thanks go to Tom Cotterell, formerly of Lipper Analytical Services, for supplying background information on mutual fund performance. Also, thanks to Robert Zweig and Eileen Smiley of the Securities and Exchange Commission for providing background materials on various SEC no-action letters. Thanks to Mike Caccese of the Association for Investment Management & Research (AIMR) for his successful efforts on behalf of investment managers to add reasonableness to the reporting of performance results, as reflected in the December 18, 1996, SEC no-action letter, described later in the text. Thanks to Ed Karppi of AIMR for checking out some of my interpretations of AIMR formulas.

Many thanks also to Cindy Kent of AIMR, Jerry Lavin of Berger Associates, Jon Edwards of Pyramid Technologies, and John

Vicini, a close friend and associate, for their continuous support and encouragement with this effort.

Many thanks to my family for putting up with my habit of departing in the early hours and weekends to devote time to completing this book.

I would also like to acknowledge all my English teachers who put up with my lack of respect for the wisdom they attempted to impart. As an undergraduate mathematics major (one who was convinced there was an inverse correlation between English and Math—who saw this as justification for not wanting to devote more time to English composition or literature), I simply lacked appreciation for the subject. Little did I know that I would spend so much time writing, and actually writing a book!

Since I'm an expert at procrastination, it was not unexpected that I missed my original due date to get my completed manuscript to the publisher. This was a rather fortuitous event, since had I made my date, I would have missed the inclusion of a recent ruling by the SEC (in the no-action letter of December 12, 1996, briefly noted above and discussed in greater detail later), which has a major bearing on the advertising and reporting of returns. The reality is that the field of performance measurement is quite expansive and dynamic. Approaches are being employed today that were unheard of a few years ago. The power of the computer is allowing us to perform unheard-of calculations that will permit us to do a better job of evaluating and reporting performance, and hopefully provide a greater assessment of how our managers are doing.

My goal in writing this book was to provide a resource that contains basic (and some not-so-basic) information on many of the aspects of performance reporting. I'm hopeful that the reader will agree that this was accomplished. There are many advanced aspects of performance, especially regarding risk and performance attribution, that weren't included. This is partly because of the vast variety of ideas and theories, and the fact that many of these ideas are still being developed. The author leaves it to the readers to search out these other areas on their own.

Hopefully, this book will serve as a reference text and instructional guide. It reflects much of what I've learned through various consulting assignments, conferences, seminars, and research.

The first chapter provides some background for the concept of performance measurement, and draws on some nonfinancial areas for comparison and, hopefully, clarification. Chapter 2 has a detailed explanation of time-weighted returns, contrasting this generally accepted approach with the older method called dollar-weighted returns. Chapter 3 provides a mix of topics relating to the calculation of returns, including a comparison between approximation methods and true time-weighted returns.

Chapter 4 introduces the concept of performance attribution, one of the fields that is undergoing increased emphasis. Chapter 5 discusses style analysis, a way of validating that managers are investing the way we think they are. Chapter 6 covers risk, an increasingly important topic given the many cases of losses due to greater risks being taken than desired by the client.

Chapter 7 discusses how the Securities and Exchange Commission has influenced performance reporting. Chapter 8 provides an overview of the various standards that have been developed since the late 1960s. Chapter 9 focuses on the standards developed by the Association for Investment Management & Research (AIMR), which have influenced most U.S. managers and many non-U.S. managers, too.

Chapter 10 provides an overview into the various ways we can compare a manager's performance. Chapter 11 gives an explanation of policies, procedures, and controls, items each money management firm should have in place to ensure accurate reporting of performance. Finally, Chapter 12 provides the author's look into the future, and how this dynamic field may be changing.

Performance is a complex but important part of a money management firm's process. I hope this reference provides you with a resource you can call upon to help with your daily activities.

ENDNOTES

1. For simplicity, I will use the term sector to refer generally to subportfolio groupings. This saves us from having to try to cover all the different levels for which we might want to calculate returns.
2. In spite of the fact that several individuals took the time to review the manuscript, any errors are, of course, mine. I've learned that no matter how many people review something, there's bound to be a mistake somewhere. I very much hope this book is an exception, but if it isn't, I apologize for any confusion it (they) may cause.
3. Titled "Youth," this quotation appears on a wall at the American Museum of Natural History in Manhattan.

I want to see you game boys. I want to see you brave and manly and I also want to see you gentle and tender.

Be practical as well as generous in your ideals. Keep your eyes on the stars and your feet on the ground. Courage, hard work, self mastery and intelligent effort are all essential to a successful life. Character in the long run is the decisive factor in the life of an individual and of nations alike.

Theodore Roosevelt[3]

CHAPTER 1

What Is Performance
Measurement?

The cartoon below serves as a metaphor for many when it comes to performance measurement, though their comments wouldn't exactly mirror those of these characters. Performance measurement often seems at times to be an extremely complicated and nebulous field.

If it makes you feel any better, these opinions are probably not too far from reality. And, unfortunately, the field has only grown in

"Oh, if only it were so simple."

Drawing by Bernard Schoenbaum; © 1987 The New Yorker Magazinre, Inc.

complexity as the simple derivation of return on investment has expanded to encompass many more calculations and disclosures.

To put it simply, performance measurement is the *measurement* of performance. The term can be used to describe the performance of many things and often is. The primary focus of this book is to discuss the measurement of performance in the money management industry, that is, the way to quantify how well a money manager has done in making investment decisions for his clients and how the market value of investments has appreciated (or depreciated) over time.

People generally love statistics, and performance measurement is a statistic that can effectively portray a manager's success. But, as we all know, statistics can be misleading, so it's important that performance be measured in a manner acceptable to the industry to avoid confusion or misrepresentation.

We'll begin by discussing performance measurement in general. A broad perspective should help acquaint you with the general concepts and challenges of measuring someone's performance. We'll also touch briefly on the present value method and how it relates to one of the earlier means of deriving performance, the internal rate of return calculation.

PERFORMANCE MEASUREMENT IN OTHER PROFESSIONS

Some professions lend themselves to a quantifiable measure of performance, while others don't. Baseball is probably one of the best examples of a profession that places a great deal of emphasis on statistics and measurement of performance. Pitchers are tracked with such things as ERA (earned-run average), win/loss percentage, innings pitched, success against right-handed batters, success against left-handed batters, etc. Batters are measured by batting average, on-base percentage, slugging percentage, and so on. Players are compensated based on their prior success, even though team owners and managers know that *past results aren't necessarily indicative of future performance.*

Law is a profession that doesn't generally lend itself to performance measurement. A lawyer might be able to tell you how many cases she has won versus how many she's lost, and if you're looking for a lawyer, this kind of statistic may be of value to you.

However, using this as a measurement tool to compare one lawyer with another might not be fair. For example, what *kinds* of cases did each lawyer have? What were the circumstances? There are so many variables to look at that this might not be an appropriate measurement or comparison tool. Is the playing field a level one?

Another profession for which statistics aren't recorded or reported is medicine. Surgeons don't report their *operations won/lost*, though some patients may want to know such information before they "go under the knife"! However, we are beginning to see independent ratings being applied to hospitals, acknowledging the need by the public to have some measure of performance.

Business managers' success can't easily be quantified. If you hear, "Mary Smith is an excellent manager," what would you think? How can this assessment be made? In most cases, managers are assessed using *non*-quantifiable criteria—pure subjective judgment.

Would you attempt to quantify the decisions a manager makes? Would you expect to hear, "oh, she's[1] not a good manager. She was wrong 27.5% of the time last year in making decisions"? Probably not.

The military is known for its efficiency reports, OERs (officer efficiency reports) and EERs (enlisted efficiency reports). These are subjective assessments of the performance of individuals that, unfortunately, are often inflated. When I was in the army, I learned that unless you were classified in the "top 10%," you were not doing very well. As you can imagine, the "top 10%" was very crowded.

Table 1–1 lists comments from some British Navy efficiency reports. Can you imagine the equivalent comments for some money managers?

ADVANTAGES OF QUANTIFIABLE MEASUREMENT TECHNIQUES

Whenever possible, quantifiable criteria should be used when assessing someone's performance. Subjective judgment is generally quite risky and open to interpretation. For example, while my assessment of a manager's performance may be based on the attitudes of his staff toward him, and yours might be influenced by the comments made by your clients, a quantifiable statistic is generally free from bias and misinterpretation.

T A B L E   1–1

Efficiency Reports[2]

The British military writes EPRs as officer fitness reports. The form used for Royal Navy and Marines fitness reports is the S206. The following are actual excerpts taken from people's 206s:

- His men would follow him anywhere, but only out of curiosity.
- I would not breed from this officer.
- This officer is really not so much of a has-been, but more of a definitely won't be.
- When she opens her mouth, it seems that this is only to change whichever foot was previously in there.
- He has carried out each and every one of his duties to his entire satisfaction.
- He would be out of his depth in a car park puddle.
- Technically sound, but socially impossible.
- This officer reminds me very much of a gyroscope—always spinning around at a frantic pace, but not really going anywhere.
- This young lady has delusions of adequacy.
- When he joined my ship, this officer was something of a granny; since then he has aged considerably.
- This medical officer has used my ship to carry his genitals from port to port, and my officers to carry him from bar to bar.
- Since my last report he has reached rock bottom, and has started to dig.
- She sets low personal standards and then consistently fails to achieve them.
- He has the wisdom of youth, and the energy of old age.
- This officer should go far—and the sooner he starts, the better.
- In my opinion, this pilot should not be authorized to fly below 250 feet.
- This man is depriving a village somewhere of an idiot.
- The only ship I would recommend this man for is citizenship.
- Works well when under constant supervision and cornered like a rat.

If you're the owner of a professional football team, you're probably more interested in the *statistics* that come with a player than the subjective assessment of others. Clearly, subjective criticism is of value, but the numbers are generally what counts the most.

Often, this subjective assessment may have to do with a player's attitude or general level of performance. Owners want to know if someone is a *team player* or a *hot dog*. A person's attitude can affect not only his performance but the performance of those around him.

INVESTMENT PERFORMANCE

People who have money to invest and are looking for professional help are more likely to be interested in the *return on their investment*, which would reflect how well a prospective manager invests clients' money, rather than what people think of the manager as a person. This is where *investment performance measurement* comes into play. This process provides statistics on the portfolio manager's prior success in investing her clients' funds.

It's critical that statistics used to measure performance adhere to certain requirements:

1. *Appropriateness*—The statistics chosen have to be appropriate for the situation. The old adage that *statistics lie* often describes the results of using the *wrong* statistic in a given situation.

2. *Consistency*—The statistics should be consistently used. Varying statistics over time will create concern (i.e., is a particular statistic used only when it's favorable?).

3. *Freedom from Bias*—The measurement must be free of bias, that is, it can't be influenced by outside or irrelevant factors.

4. *Standardization*—There should be universal agreement in the use of a given measurement. Often, at the early stages, there may be multiple ways to measure a particular event. Over time, participants tend to settle on the measurement (or measurements) that should be employed. This ensures that everyone is using the same *yardstick* in measuring performance.

Often, people use statistics that make them look the best (or someone else look the worst).[3] This is when having standards can be very helpful. If *everyone* is using the same *yardstick*, "game playing"[4] can be minimized.

BASIC CONCEPT—PRESENT VALUE OF MONEY

Before we actually discuss rates of return, I think it would be helpful to briefly touch on the topic of the *present value of money*. These calculations can be thought of as the basis for many of the formulas we'll use, so it's helpful to spend a moment on them.

The concept of *present value* comes into play when one is attempting to analyze various investment opportunities. For example, if we could have $1,217 at the end of 5 years or $1,000 today to invest at 4% annually for 5 years, which should we choose? Well, if the $1,000 was invested in a savings program paying a 4% dividend, it would increase to $1,217 in 5 years, due to compounding, as shown in Table 1–2.

You should be indifferent between having $1,000 invested at 4% or receiving $1,217 in 5 years, since you'll end up with the same amount. The $1,000 is the *present value* of $1,217 in 5 years when the applicable interest rate is 4%.

When an investment appreciates in value, it can do so in a rather simple fashion, such as having a value added to it on a regular basis (for example, starting with a dollar and having a dime added to it at regular intervals):

$$\$1.00, 1.10, 1.20, 1.30, ...$$

If we receive income based on our investment, and if we reinvest our income so as to receive income on our income, we will have compounded growth. The following series shows an investment receiving a 10% return with compounding:

$$\$1.00, 1.10, 1.21, 1.33, ...$$

The future value is the value at some point in the future of some investment that is subject to compound growth. Knowing the amount we're investing and the growth rate, we can determine the future value of our investment at some future date by using the classic formula:

T A B L E   1–2

Present Value Example

Year	Beginning Amount P_0	* (1 + .I)	Ending Value P_1
1	$1,000	1.04	$1,040
2	$1,040	1.04	$1,081
3	$1,081	1.04	$1,125
4	$1,125	1.04	$1,170
5	$1,170	1.04	$1,217

$$P_i = P_0(1 + i)^t$$

where

P_0 = the starting principal, or our initial investment
P_i = the future principal, or future value of our investment
i = the interest rate, or our compound income rate
t = the period over which the interest is compounded

Going back to our earlier example, if we invest $1,000 for a 5-year period with interest compounded annually at 4%, our formula becomes:

$$P_1 = 1,000 \cdot (1 + 0.04)^t = 1,000 \cdot (1.04)^5 = \$1,217$$

Alternatively, if the interest rate is 10%, the formula becomes:

$$P_1 = 1,000 \cdot (1 + 0.10)^t = 1,000 \cdot (1.10)^5 = \$1,611$$

At a 10% annual rate of return, our $1,000 investment will become $1,611 in 5 years, so $1,000 is the present value of $1,611 in 5 years when the applicable interest rate is 10 percent.

Prior to the availability of calculators and personal computers, present value tables would be used to determine either the present or future value of money invested at a given interest rate. Please refer to Appendix F for a brief discussion of how the present value table can be used.

INTERNAL RATE OF RETURN

In our earlier example, we know the present value, income rate, and time period to solve for the future value. Now we want to solve for the income rate, knowing the other variables. To do this, we use the internal rate of return (IRR), which is related to the present value concept. Here, we use the following formula:

$$Present\ value = \frac{future\ value}{1 + i} + \frac{future\ value}{(1 + i)^2} + \frac{future\ value}{(1 + i)^3}$$

Solving for i requires an iterative ("trial and error") process. Knowing the *present value* and *future values* (cash flows), we select values for i until we find the right one. Once we find a value that solves this equation, we've determined our income rate. This will be our internal rate of return.

Let's take a simple example, where we invest $1,000 and receive $250 income each year for 3 years. What is our internal rate of return?

The formula is constructed as above:

$$\$1,000 = \frac{\$250}{1 + i} + \frac{\$250}{(1 + i)^2} + \frac{\$250}{(1 + i)^3} + \frac{\$250}{(1 + i)^4} + \frac{\$250}{(1 + i)^5}$$

We choose values of i until we solve the equation. Once we do, we've obtained the IRR. Table 1–3 shows an iterative process that arrives at the solution.

We need to find a rate that will yield a total of $1,000 (our investment amount). We first try 10 percent. This yields a value of $947.70, which is too low, so we must try a lower rate. Next, we try 7%, which yields a value of $1,025.05. This is too high, so we try 8%, which yields $998.18—much closer to our target. After some further attempts, the value of 7.93% comes pretty close to our goal, so our IRR is approximately 7.93%.

Investments don't always mirror this kind of model (where we lay out a certain amount and receive payments back over a set number of years). We need other ways to derive the rate of return for our investment. In chapter 2, we'll discuss the internal rate of return (IRR) method of deriving rates of return in a bit more detail, plus other methods to derive returns. For now, you should be able to see how this formula ties back to the present value method.

T A B L E   1–3

Finding the Internal Rate of Return

Year	Beginning Income	Amount 10%	7%	8%	Ending Value 7.93%
1	$250	227.27	233.64	231.48	231.63
2	$250	206.61	218.36	214.33	214.61
3	$250	187.83	204.07	198.46	198.84
4	$250	170.75	190.72	183.76	184.23
5	$250	155.23	178.25	170.15	170.70
	Totals:	$947.70	$1025.05	$998.18	$1000.02

MEASURING INVESTMENT PERFORMANCE— THE SIMPLEST CASE

A very simple example shows how we might approach the measurement of a money manager's investment skill. On January 1, you gave someone $1,000 to invest. It's now a month later and you hear that your account is valued at $1,100. How well have you done?

Well, you have $100 more than you started with. What would you tell people who asked you how well you did *in the market* last month? Would you say, "my portfolio manager made $100 for me last month"? You could, but what meaning would that have.

Let's say you were speaking with a friend who also hired a money manager at the beginning of the month. That friend gave her manager $2,000, and at the end of the month the account was worth $2,100. She may respond "I made $100 too." Is that good? Did you do equally well, or did one of you actually do better than the other?

Let's take a closer look at this situation. You and your friend each made $100 on your individual investments, but you put up $1,000 while your friend invested $2,000. Do you think you both would have made $100 if you had reversed money managers, that is, if you had given your money to your friend's manager, and vice versa? Probably not.

Rather than look at the *amount* of money you made, it's better to look at the *rate of return* you received on your investment. The Rate of Return, or ROR, is a percentage that reflects the amount of change that took place in your investment.

A simple way to calculate the ROR is to divide the amount you made by the initial investment:

$$ROR = \frac{Amount\ Made}{Initial\ Investment}$$

This calculation will give us a decimal number. This number is then typically multiplied by 100 in order to state it as a percentage.[5]

In your case, you started with $1,000 and ended the month with $1,100. If we divide the amount you made by the amount you started with, we'll see that you had a 10% improvement in the value of your assets.

$$ROR_{you} = \frac{Amount\ Made}{Initial\ Investment} = \frac{\$100}{\$1,000} = 0.10 = 10\%$$

Your friend, who made $100 on a $2,000 investment, had a 5% return.

$$ROR_{your\ friend} = \frac{Amount\ Made}{Initial\ Investment} = \frac{\$100}{\$2,000} = 0.05 = 5\%$$

Had you switched money managers, all things being equal (that is, you each got the same investment return), you would have probably made only $50, while your friend would have made $200.[6]

If you were to *rank* these two managers by looking at the rates of return rather than the dollar amounts generated, you would probably feel that your manager *outperformed* your friend's. After all, you got a 10% return while your friend only got a 5% return. As you'll see in later chapters, you need more than just the ROR to compare managers, and, as you'll see in chapter 2, the ROR formula can be much more complex than the one we've used here.

HANDLING LOSSES

What happens if you *lose* money rather than *make* money on your investment? The same approach that is used for measuring the rate of return for gains is used for measuring losses. Let's again use an example to demonstrate how this works.

You have a second friend who invested $1,000 with another money manager. At the end of the month, he has only $900 left. In other words, he lost $100. What's his ROR?

Here, we divide the amount he lost by the starting value to see that he had a −10% ROR:

$$ROR_{friend\#2} = \frac{Amount\ Made}{Initial\ Investment} = \frac{-\$100}{\$1,000} = -0.10 = -10\%$$

In other words, he suffered a 10% loss on his investment.

STANDARD NOTATION FOR FORMULAS

Now we're going to start to use more *standard notation* in our formulas. The general formula for what we've done so far is:

$$ROR = \left[\frac{(EMV - BMV)}{BMV} \right] *100,$$

where

ROR = rate of return (stated as a percent)
EMV = ending market value
BMV = beginning market value

We've been using the term "Amount Made (or lost)." The expression "EMV – BMV" gives us this same information. For example, in your case, you started with $1,000 and ended with $1,100. The initial value ($1,000) is the beginning market value, or BMV. The ending value ($1,100) is the ending market value, or EMV. The amount made is the difference (EMV – BMV), or in your case, $1,100 – $1,000, or $100.

USING RATES OF RETURN TO COMPARE MANAGERS

As the example suggested earlier, knowing the ROR your friends received can be used to estimate the increase or decrease in money they would have made for you had you given them your money to invest. If we expand our list a bit, we can do a further comparison (see Table 1–4).

We're showing seven different managers, with investing success ranging from a high of 30% to a low of minus 25%. To assess how well you would have done[7] with your $1,000 investment,

T A B L E   1–4

Manager	ROR	EMV
Manager Comparison BMV = $1,000		
A	30%	$1,300
B	15%	$1,150
C	8%	$1,080
D	0%	$1,000
E	–5%	$950
F	–10%	$900
G	–25%	$750

simply multiply the rate of return (in decimal format) by the investment amount, and then add it to (or subtract it from) the initial investment.

Here, we see that in the best case you would have made $300, while in the worst case, you would have lost $250.[8]

Is that all there is ...?

At first glance, this seems like a pretty simple subject. After all, if all we need to do is take the amount of money we made during the period and divide it by the amount we started with, what could be simpler?

Well, performance measurement is quite a bit more complicated than this, as you'll see in the subsequent chapters. For example, here we showed three cases where the amount of money that was invested stayed the same from the beginning to the end of the measurement period. This is often not the case. Investors often *add to* or *take away from* their initial investment. The money that's added is typically referred to as a *contribution* or *inflow*. Money taken away is generally called a *withdrawal* or *outflow*. Together, we refer to these activities as *cash flows*. Cash flows can have a dramatic effect on performance, and the formula we've used above simply won't work when cash flows occur. Chapter 2 will go into this matter in greater detail.

For our purposes at this time, this brief introduction should give you the general sense of how performance is measured.

PERFORMANCE MEASUREMENT ABUSES

Some managers have made performance measurement an *art* and have found ways to make their performance look better than it should. In an article titled "How a Money Manager Can Pull a Rabbit Out of a Hat,"[9] James White points out some of the lengths managers will go to to present superior performance. His opening paragraph sets the stage: "Too many money managers use smoke and mirrors to make their performance look better." While I would argue that this statement is a bit strong, there have been cases of abuse and misrepresentation of performance results. To suggest that this problem is widespread and common would be a mistake. I believe that even Mr. White would agree that most money managers are fair and honest in their reporting.

In spite of the caveat that *past performance isn't a guarantee of future results,* managers rely very heavily on performance results to attract new clients. This pressure has caused managers to put their results in the "best possible light." We often read of cases where managers mislead clients by being too aggressive in the positioning of their past performance.

"Managers have developed a bag of tricks to levitate their performance figures. The magic includes having investment records instantly appear where none existed before; making poorly performing accounts that drag down performance simply vanish, and causing the same investment record to appear in two places at once."

Mr. White briefly discusses four of the ways managers can stretch their performance results:

Back Testing: This approach has been used by firms that employ *quantitative* techniques in their investment practice. Here, managers apply a methodology against historical information to derive the supposed returns they *would have received* had this method been implemented in the past.

Some of the problems with this practice are obvious. A firm will be *creating* returns based on 20/20 hindsight. Most critics of this practice believe that you'll never see back-tested results that weren't superior. (Wouldn't we all have been out of the market on October 19th, 1987?)[10]

Portable Records: This practice occurs when a manager (or managers) leaves one firm to join or start another. Occasionally, they'll want to take their performance records with them.

There's nothing wrong with this, as long as they were 100% responsible for the record and take all the aspects of the investment/analysis process with them. However, if their decisions were based on analysis done by others in the firm, and those individuals won't be coming, or if they were adhering to certain policies dictated by the firm in general, such portability is probably inappropriate. See chapter 7 for further discussion on this.

Model Portfolios: Managers don't often have the control they'd like over their client accounts. Some clients impose restrictions on the securities a manager can purchase. For example, they may disallow "sin stocks."[11] Others add or remove money at varying times, causing the manager to have to buy or sell securities at less than ideal times. And others require managers to trade all or a portion of their account with one or more selected brokers. These constraints can influence a manager's performance results.

What's the solution? Create an account that can't be affected by a client—create a *model* portfolio. Such a portfolio would be controlled by the firm and would reflect the trade decisions the manager feels are appropriate, without client constraints.

However, there are flaws with this approach. First, it's a *paper portfolio*, and as such, isn't *real*. Second, it creates an opportunity for manipulation (e.g., a "buy" at the beginning of the month didn't turn out very well by the end of the month, so we'll remove it from the model; we missed an opportunity to "sell" a particular security a week ago, so we'll insert it now).

There are no "official" records kept by a third party (e.g., custodial or brokerage statements) as there would be with real accounts. This leaves room for tampering or the application of 20/20 hindsight.

Survivorship: Why do clients leave managers? There can be a variety of reasons, but often it's because the manager didn't perform to the client's liking (i.e., his performance wasn't very good).

Some managers want to show performance only for accounts that are still active (i.e., drop the complete history for accounts that have left, which is called "survivorship bias"). The result: the manager will be getting rid of the poorly performing accounts and increasing her overall return.

Other games have been played in an effort to make performance look better. At the time of Mr. White's article, there were no industry standards for how managers should report performance to prospective clients. Now, there are.

We'll take this up in chapter 9.

THE GROWING IMPORTANCE OF ACCURATE PERFORMANCE NUMBERS

The investment industry has been aware for some time that there are managers who will *stretch the truth* or commit out-and-out fraud[12] in order to make their performance look better and secure new business.

The New York Times reported a case where a manager's superior returns were being heralded until it was learned that they were far from accurate.[13] It seems that one of the firm's employees erroneously reversed the sign on securities with negative returns (but didn't reverse the sign of those with positive returns), resulting in very high rates of return. The return that was initially reported for 1985 was 46.5%. When it was corrected, it dropped to 8.8%. This error was discovered when the firm recalculated their numbers in order to comply with the Association for Investment Management & Research's Performance Presentation Standards (AIMR-PPS™).

Observers wondered why the manager didn't know of the error, given such a wide difference. Portfolio managers typically have a *general* idea of how they're doing, and a 37.7% overstatement is something most managers would probably be aware of.

Since the late 1960s, various standards have been developed that are meant to establish consistency in calculating returns. The reality is that people can still *cheat*. Fortunately, the Securities and Exchange Commission (SEC) periodically reviews managers to check such things. There have been several cases of managers who have been taken to court because of their failure to provide accurate returns.

Since the mid- to late 1980s, there's been increased attention to the whole topic of performance measurement. It has grown to incorporate such things as *performance attribution* (see chapter 4) and *risk measurement* (see chapter 6).

PAST PERFORMANCE IS NO GUARANTEE OF FUTURE RESULTS

Many people are familiar with the disclaimer, "past performance is no guarantee of future results." After all it (or something like it) appears in any advertisement reporting a firm's rate of return. It's intention is to keep money managers from aggressively selling future business on past success and to caution investors against assuming that the returns a manager produced last year will be repeated in years to come. The SEC requires such a disclaimer on mutual fund advertising.

Just because a manager was very successful in the past is no assurance that he will repeat this success. There have been several managers who have had one good year and mediocre performance during the rest of the time. To assume that a manager will repeat successful performance is risky, in most cases.

Nevertheless, we're all interested in knowing past performance, because we do anticipate that there will be some level of consistency. Our earlier baseball example is a case in point. Team owners anticipate that a player will perform at a level consistent with the prior year's. This is why a player will attempt to renegotiate a contract following an exceptionally good year, even though the likelihood of a repeat may be questionable. Investors, too, expect some level of consistency from year-to-year, even though one can probably argue that an investor has a lot less control then a ball player does.

CHAPTER SUMMARY

In this chapter, we've introduced the basic concept of performance measurement. This concept is not limited to the investment industry but is, in fact, part of many different professions. We've explained the importance of using statistics to measure performance. A simple formula was used to show how performance can be calculated. We also discussed the net present value method and showed how it ties in with the internal rate of return. Hopefully, you're now ready to delve into more complicated methods of assessing performance.

ENDNOTES

1. In an effort to be fair, I will attempt to alternate the use of "he" and "she" throughout this book.
2. This list was provided to the author by a friend, who obtained it indirectly from the Internet. Consequently, the original source is unknown.
3. An example might help: An incumbent mayor says "more people are employed in our city today than ever before." His opponent claims "we have the highest unemployment rate in our city's history." Who's right?
   Well, both could be. If the city has undergone significant growth in its population, it's possible that more people are employed than in the past. It's also possible that the percentage of people out of work is higher than ever before. Confusion can arise from the use of inconsistent measurements.
4. At various times, I'll use the term *playing games* or *game playing*. By this I mean the employment of techniques or strategies to manipulate the information being presented, in order to make a presentation more favorable. On occasion, money managers have been known to *play games* in order to make their performance results stand out and come across better than they would otherwise.
5. For example, instead of saying your return was 0.235, you would multiply the decimal by 100 and say your return was 23.5 percent. Instead of saying your portfolio was up 0.05, you'd say it was up 5%.
6. If you had a 5% return on your $1,000 investment, you would have made $50; your friend would have had a $200 return on a 10% rate.

7. It's worth emphasizing the expression *would have done*. As discussed later in this chapter, *past performance is no guarantee of future results*. Consequently, it wouldn't be appropriate to use the results in this table as a predictor of future returns. Here, we're using these statistics only to show how an investor *would have done* had she had her money with the various managers.

8. Not only are prior period *rates of return* not necessarily good predictors of future performance, they're also no guarantee that you would have obtained the stated *ROR* had you invested with that manager. This is because *reported* rates of return are typically *averages* of a group of returns. It's conceivable that *no one* obtained the reported return!

   Plus, in most cases, approximately half of the manager's clients had returns *above* the reported return, while the other half had returns *below* the return since, again, the reported return is an *average*.

   For example, a manager has four clients with returns as follows: 10%, 12%, 14%, 16%. The average return he would report would be 13% [(10+12+14+16)/4 = 13]. No one in this group actually had a 13% return, and two accounts were above the average while two were below).

   Nevertheless, it's common to go through an exercise like this to *estimate* what you would have obtained in performance for a reported period.

9. White [1989], page C1.

10. This is the date of a major *adjustment* in the value of the stock market. On that date, the market dropped 508 points, or 22.6% in value.

11. "Sin stocks" typically refers to companies that are involved in gambling, tobacco, and alcohol, though it can be expanded to include other industries that are found unacceptable to the client.

12. A recent case appeared in the November 20, 1996, issue of *The New York Times*. In "Investment Adviser Admits $65 Million Fraud Against Her Clients" Laurence Zuckerman reported on Teresa V. Fernandez, who had managed to bilk clients of millions while operating an advisory firm out of her home. She distributed false statements that reflected somewhat *overstated* performance results, while in fact she was stealing her clients' money.

13. Antilla [1993].

CHAPTER 2

Time-Weighted Rates of Return

In this chapter, we'll contrast *time-weighted* and *dollar-weighted* rates of return. We'll expand on our earlier discussion on the internal rate of return and introduce several other methods of assessing performance.

The reader is cautioned not to be overly concerned with the formula we'll introduce for the internal rate of return. Its complexity can be a bit humbling, but rest assured it's here primarily for completeness and historical perspective, not as a recommended approach for deriving performance results.

DOLLAR-WEIGHTED RATES OF RETURN

Before 1968, most money managers used the internal rate of return (IRR) formula to calculate performance. The IRR is calculated by assuming that each dollar grows at the same constant rate and by finding that rate. This is done at a specified frequency of compounding.[1]

We briefly introduced the IRR in chapter 1. Please recall that this formula relates to the Present Value formula, which is used to determine either the present value of some known future value, given an interest or income rate, or the future value given a present value and rate.

The IRR solves for the rate, given known present and future values. The formula that was introduced in chapter 1 works well when we know the income flows that will occur as a result of our investment (e.g., invest $1,000 and receive payments of $250 per year for the next 5 years).

$$Present\ value = \frac{future\ value}{1 + i} + \frac{future\ value}{(1 + i)^2} + \frac{future\ value}{(1 + i)^3}$$

While this has applicability to many investment scenarios, it is limited overall. Consequently, a variation is needed that will provide performance results for the general situation. The following formula satisfies this need,

$$V_0 + \sum_{j=1}^{n} C_j e^{-it_j} - V_{n+1} e^{-it_{n+1}} = 0,$$

where

V_0 = the value of the fund at the beginning of the period
C_j = the jth cash flow into or out of the fund during the period, for $j = 1, ..., n$ (an inflow [contribution] is shown as a positive number; an outflow [withdrawal] as a negative number)
V_{n+1} = the value of the fund at the end of the period
t_j = the time in years from the beginning of the period to the jth cash flow, $j = 1, ..., n$ (the symbol t_{n+1} denotes the time from the beginning to the end of the period)
i = the internal rate of return expressed as an annual rate, assuming continuous compounding[2]

The IRR is also referred to as the *dollar-weighted rate of return*. The dollar-weighted ROR is that value of the interest rate (or discount rate) i that satisfies the equation.

As noted above, this formula assumes continuous compounding. If, instead, we assume periodic or discrete compounding (e.g., annual), the IRR is represented by the following formula:

$$V_0 + \sum_{j=1}^{n} C_j (1 + r)^{-t_j} - V_{n+1} (1 + r)^{-t_{n+1}} = 0,$$

where

V_0 = the fund's value at the beginning of the period
C_1 = the net cash flow at the beginning of the second
         year, and so on until C_n
V_{n+1} = the fund's value at the end of the second year $(n + 1)$
r = the internal rate of return that satisfies the equation

These two equations define an internal rate of return to be a constant rate that makes the present value of all benefits (the fund's final value and all withdrawals from the fund) equal to the present value of all costs (the fund's initial value and all contributions). Here are some examples that should clarify some of the shortcomings of the IRR, or dollar-weighted ROR.

Example 1
We start with $1.00. During the first year, we realize a 10% return. In year two, we realize a return of 40%. No cash flows occur. Consequently, the value of the fund at the end of the first year is $1.10, and it is $1.54 at the end of the second year. The dollar-weighted ROR is found by substituting these values into the second equation, yielding:

$$1.00 - \frac{1.54}{(1 + r)^2} = 0.$$

By solving for r, we calculate an annual ROR of 24.1%.

Example 2
This example is the same as the first, with the exception that we get a cash flow of $1.00 at the beginning of the second year. So, we start with $1.00 and have $1.10 at the end of the first year. We start the second year with $2.10 (since we got an inflow of $1.00) and have $2.94 at the end of the second year. Using the second formula we have:

$$1.00 + \frac{1.00}{(1 + r)} - \frac{2.94}{(1 + r)^2} = 0.$$

Solving for r, we calculate the annual ROR to be 28.6%.[3]
    As we can see, the cash flow in the second year has caused a 2.5% increase in the ROR. And yet, the performance of the manag-

er during each of these years has not changed (10% in the first, 40% in the second). Clearly, the manager's performance has benefited from this cash flow—something he had no control over. Is this appropriate? Obviously not.

There are two glaring problems with the IRR. First, it is a nontrivial formula. Solving for r is an iterative process, where values are substituted until the formula is solved. If this were to be done by hand, much effort would have to be expended. Today, we have calculators and computers that can derive this number rather quickly. However, prior to 1968, most of the computers that could do these calculations were quite large and expensive—out of reach for most money managers.

The second and probably the more important problem is that the result is affected by cash flows. The idea behind performance measurement is to measure the performance of the *manager* and the things she has control over. Since a manager can't control the timing or amounts of contributions or withdrawals, how can we reward (or penalize) her depending on the frequency and amounts of these flows?

CASH FLOWS

Before we begin our discussion of time-weighted rates of return, let's spend a few moments discussing cash flows. At times, there is confusion as to what *is* or *isn't* a cash flow. A few examples would help.

A *contribution* of additional funds into an account is a cash flow. For example, when we add $1,000 to an existing account, we treat these funds as a cash flow. The $1,000 is a cash flow. Our initial investment is also technically a cash flow, but we normally consider it to be our starting position.[4]

What if we gave our manager securities that were worth $1,000 rather than cash, would this be a cash flow? Yes. When securities are moved into an account, they are valued on the date of their deposit, and this amount is recorded as a cash flow.

What if I originally paid $2,000 for these securities, but they were worth $1,000 when they were given to the money manager, would the flow be $2,000 or $1,000? It would be $1,000—the value at the time of the deposit. Your *tax basis*[5] for the securities is $2,000, but the manager's performance will be measured against their value at the time of their movement into the account.

Treatment of Income

Income refers to money that is paid by securities. Income can be taxable or nontaxable.[6] For performance measurement purposes, the tax status is generally not taken into consideration. Examples of income are bond interest and stock dividends.

One of the securities in my portfolio pays a $50 dividend. Is this a cash flow? No, not if it stays in the portfolio. In this case, it's treated as an *appreciation* in the value of the portfolio. However, if you ask that *income* be *distributed* rather than *reinvested,* then it is a cash flow, but *out of* the portfolio.

Let's take a *very* simple example to demonstrate this situation. Your portfolio consists of only one security that was purchased for $100. It pays a $5 dividend. You've directed your manager to *distribute* your income, so you get a check for $5. At the end of the period, your portfolio is worth $100. What was your return?

Some might conclude zero, since you ended up with what you started with—$100. But, you also made $5 that you need to account for. It's appropriate to give your manager credit for picking the security that paid this income.

Capital Gains

A manager sold a security that was purchased for $100 for $120— is this $20 a cash flow? No—it's a capital gain. During the life of your portfolio, many securities will be bought and sold. From a performance measurement perspective, we don't care about these intermittent transactions. What we are concerned with is the value of the portfolio at the end of various *measurement periods.* The *result* of these transactions will be reflected in the ending period market values.

If your portfolio consisted only of that one security that's valued at $100, and at the end of the period the manager sells it for $120, you will have $120 in cash sitting in your portfolio. Thus, your return for the period is 20%. If, on the other hand, the manager didn't sell the security, we would still measure the *value* of the asset at the end of the period. All things being equal, the security would be *valued* at around $120, again resulting in a 20% ROR. The difference is that in the first example, you made $20, while in the second, you have a *paper profit* of $20.[7]

INTRODUCTION TO TIME-WEIGHTED RATES OF RETURN

The event that occurred in 1968 that changed the way managers calculate performance was the introduction of calculation standards by the Bank Administration Institute (BAI). Their publication, *Measuring the Investment Performance of Pension Funds*, had a major impact on the way firms measure performance. They pointed out the shortcomings of the IRR, or dollar-weighted, method and recommended the use of *time-weighted* formulas.

Time-weighted returns show the value of one dollar invested in a portfolio or sector for the entire period, while dollar-weighted returns show an average return of all the dollars in the portfolio or sector for the period. The dollar-weighted return reconciles the beginning dollar plus cash flows with the ending value. Time-weighted returns ignore cash flows and only look at the money that's in the fund during the period.[8]

The BAI standards, as they were to become known, were based on a seminal book written by Peter O. Dietz, titled *Pension Funds, Measuring Investment Performance*, that was published in 1966. This was Peter Dietz's Ph.D. thesis and called for the use of time-weighted returns.

Peter Dietz introduced a couple of approaches to deriving a time-weighted ROR. One was the *linked internal rate of return*. It was subsequently offered by the BAI as a method that could be used for time-weighting. The method requires the following:

1. Divide the time span for which the return is to be estimated into periods. Ideally, each cash flow should serve as a subperiod boundary.
2. Value the portfolio for each subperiod.
3. Compute the IRR for each subperiod. This requires knowing the portfolio's market value at the beginning and end of each subperiod, and the timing of cash flows during each period.

While the BAI document called for finding an "appropriate" average of these IRRs by deriving the arithmetic mean of the rates of the subperiods, it seems more appropriate to *link* the subperiod returns using geometric linking.[9]

The *Linked IRR* yields a time-weighted rate of return; it eliminates the impact of cash flows and provides a return that measures the performance of the manager. But the calculation still requires an iterative process, which was a challenge for many investment advisory firms in the late '60s and early '70s. While banks, which had large computers, could easily adopt these standards, a simpler formula was needed for investment advisers—one that didn't require the use of a powerful computer.

THE ICAA METHOD

In 1971, the Investment Counsel Association of America (ICAA) published their *Standards of Measurement and Use for Investment Performance Data*. This document offered a rather simplified formula for deriving a time-weighted ROR. The ICAA supported the BAI's findings and stated "A portfolio manager has no control over either the timing or the size of cash flows, and therefore, measuring the growth of market value alone is not a satisfactory quantitative technique on which to evaluate a manager's performance. Instead a method which eliminates the effects of external cash flows should be used."[10]

At the time the ICAA standards were introduced, most independent investment advisers[11] couldn't comply with the BAI formula because computers were needed to perform the rather complex calculations. These firms simply didn't have access to such expensive calculation machines. The BAI method was primarily for banks with large mainframe computers, while the ICAA was for investment counsel firms, which, in the early 1970s, had no computers (the PC was 10 years away).

The ICAA recognized that the time-weighted rate of return provides the required measurement. The ICAA felt that the time-weighted ROR was "appropriate for use in making investment result comparisons among total portfolios, segments of portfolios, and market indices as long as their characteristics and investment objectives are similar."[12,13]

At the time the ICAA introduced their formula, it was uncommon for portfolios to be priced on a daily[14] or even weekly basis, due to the unavailability of accurate prices and the costs involved in getting securities prices (portfolios were usually valued monthly or quarterly). Consequently, the ICAA felt that an approximate method was adequate, and they offered the following formula:

$$R = \frac{EMV - BMV - C + I}{BMV + 0.5 \cdot C}$$

where

BMV = beginning period market value
EMV = ending period market value (including reinvested income)
C = net cash flows that occurred during the period (from any source, including reinvested income)
I = total measurement period income
R = rate of return

Unlike the other formulas we'll be discussing, the ICAA includes income in the cash flow value. At the time the ICAA formula was developed, most investment advisors relied on custodial bank statements to keep track of client holdings. Accurate income figures weren't always available, so estimated amounts were calculated. This is part of the reason behind this inclusion of income in the formula.

Ideally, a calculation would be done whenever a cash flow occurs. This would produce a very accurate return value. However, as noted above, securities weren't typically priced on a daily basis. Instead, they were often priced monthly or quarterly. The ICAA formula recognizes this. It therefore assumes that all cash flows occur in the middle of the period, thus yielding an *approximation* for the *true time-weighted rate of return*.[15] The "0.5" in the denominator is used to place all cash flows in midperiod.

Here's an example to demonstrate the ICAA formula. An account starts the period with $1,000 and ends with $1,175. Included in the $175 market value appreciation is $50 in income. There's also been a $75 contribution. Our formula values are:

BMV = $1,000
EMV = $1,175
C = $125 ($75 contribution plus $50 in reinvested income)
I = $50

$$R = \frac{\$1,175 - \$1,000 - \$125 + \$50}{\$1,000 + 0.5 \cdot \$125} = \frac{100}{1062.5} = 0.0941 = 9.41\%$$

The rate of return for this example is 9.41 percent.

THE DIETZ METHOD

In an article written with Jeannette R. Kirschman,[16] Peter Dietz introduced another approximation method, referred to as the *Dietz method*. Like the ICAA formula, it is a much more simplified approach than the Linked IRR for deriving an approximate rate of return. The formula is

$$R = \left(\frac{EMV - 0.5C}{BMV + 0.5C} - 1\right) * 100$$

where

    BMV = beginning market value
    EMV = ending market value
    C = net cash flows
    R = rate of return

Like the ICAA method, the Dietz formula assumes that all cash flows occur in the middle of the measurement period (as reflected by the "0.5" factors in both the denominator and the numerator).

One difference between the Dietz method (and for that matter, the other methods we'll be discussing) and the ICAA method is that income is not a stand-alone element. Nor is reinvested income treated as a cash flow. Instead, any income that's received will be reflected only in the beginning and ending market values.[17] If income is paid out, then it will be treated as an outflow.

Using the example from above, we calculate the ROR using the Dietz method as follows:

$$R = \left(\frac{\$1{,}175 - 0.5 \cdot \$75 - 1}{\$1{,}000 + 0.5 \cdot \$75}\right) \cdot 100 = \left(\frac{\$1{,}137.5 - 1}{\$1{,}307.5}\right) \cdot 100$$
$$= (1.0964.1) \cdot 100 = 9.64\%$$

Here, the cash flow value doesn't include the income of $50, just the contribution ($75). This is why we find a slight difference in returns between this formula and the ICAA method (9.64% vs. 9.41%).

Like the ICAA method, this approach assumes that all cash flows occur at the midpoint of the measurement period. We will refer to this method as the *Dietz midpoint method (or formula).*[18]

Any midpoint method (e.g., the ICAA or the Dietz midpoint) assumes that the change in market value from the beginning to the

end of the period moved in a linear fashion, with the cash flows occurring at the halfway point (see Figure 2–1).

The reality, of course, is that the market fluctuates quite a bit
(see Figure 2–2).

Contributions are assumed to be in the portfolio for half the
period, when in reality they may have been in for just a few days
or for most of the month. Likewise, in the case of outflows, the
money is assumed to be in the portfolio for half the month, but it
may have departed early in the month or at the end of the month.
Such assumptions can erode the accuracy of the resulting return.

Dietz and Kirschman recognized the shortcomings of the *mid-point* methods and offered an alternative that is somewhat more accurate: a *day-weighting* formula. Rather than assume that all flows occur
at midmonth, thus giving the manager credit for having the flow for
half the month, this formula places the money in the portfolio for only
that portion of the month when the manager actually had control of it.
This formula is often referred to as the *modified Dietz method.*

F I G U R E   2–1

Market Assumptions

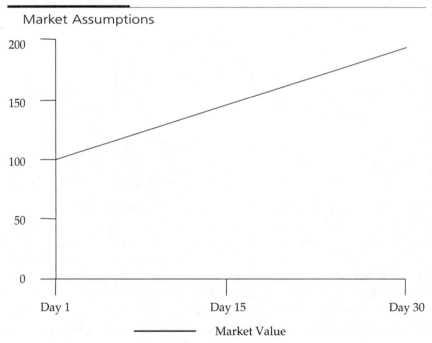

Market Value

F I G U R E   2–2

Market Realities

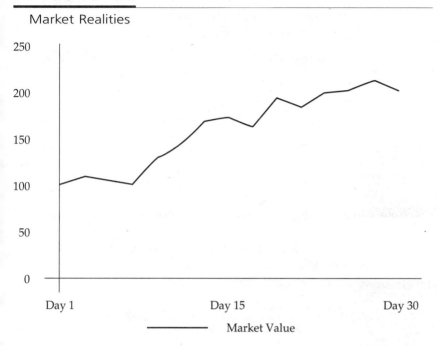

Market Value

For example, if a contribution is made on the fifth day of the month, rather than assume that the manager only had the money available for 15 days (in a 30-day month), the formula should more accurately place the money in the portfolio for 25 days. Likewise, if an outflow occurred on the fifth, assuming the money was in the account till the 15th would penalize the manager (since the return would presume a larger amount of money being available to invest than was actually the case).

The modified Dietz formula is essentially the same as the *midpoint* method, with the exception that the "0.5" multiplier is replaced. We need to introduce a new expression:

$$W_i = \frac{CD - D_i}{CD}$$

where

W_i = the proportion of the total number of days in the period the cash flow has been in (or out) of the portfolio

CD = the total number of calendar days in the period
D = the total number of days since the beginning of the
            period in which the cash flow F_i occurred

So, if the measurement period is the month of June (30 days), and the flow occurred on the 5th,

$$W_i = \frac{30 - 5}{30} = \frac{25}{30} = 0.833$$

the formula becomes

$$R = \left(\frac{EMV - (1 - WD) \cdot C}{BMV + WD \cdot C} - 1 \right) \cdot 100$$

Here's a simple example to show how this *day weighting* can alter a portfolio's return.

We begin with $10,000 and get a $1,000 contribution on the 10th of the month. We end the month at $12,050. Using the midpoint method, we get the following result:

$$R = \left(\frac{\$12,050 - 0.5 \cdot (\$1,000)}{\$10,000 + 0.5 \cdot (\$1,000)} - 1 \right) \cdot 100 = 10.0\%.$$

The day-weighting method, however, yields the following

$$R = \left(\frac{\$12,050 - \left(1 - \dfrac{30 - 10}{30} \right) \cdot (\$1,000) - 1}{\$10,000 + \left(\dfrac{30 - 10}{30} \right) \cdot (\$1,000)} \right) \cdot 100 = 9.84\%.$$

The midpoint method assumed the manager had the money for half the month (15 days). In reality, he had it for 20 days. This additional 5 days caused the return to drop 16 basis points.[19] This makes intuitive sense; since the manager had the money longer, a higher return could have been realized.

The decision to *day-weight* a period's return is often based on the size of the cash flow. Large flows (generally thought of as being greater than 10% of the account's market value)[20] tend to cause the greatest distortion in the resulting rate of return. If an organization is using a *midpoint* formula, it's generally advisable to *day-weight* if the net *absolute value* of the cash flows equals or exceeds 10% of the beginning period market value. It will result in a more accurate ROR.[21]

Absolute value is a mathematical term, where all values are expressed as a positive number, even if their nonabsolute value is negative. It is expressed mathematically by placing vertical lines on either side of the original term, for example:

$$|5| = 5$$

$$|-5| = 5$$

In other words, the absolute value of 5 is 5, as is the absolute value of negative 5.

So, to determine if our cash flows exceed 10% of the starting market value, we would take the absolute value of each day's cash flow,[22] sum these values, and compare the sum with 10% of the market value. For example, our starting value is $1,000. A "large" flow would exceed 10% of this number, or $100. We've had the following flows in the month:

January 3 = +$10 (absolute value = 10)
January 7 = +$15 (15)
January 10 = −$20 (20)
January 20 = +30 (30)
January 27 = +30 (30)

The sum of the absolute values is 105, which exceeds $100 or 10%. Therefore, we would want to use the modified formula when calculating the return for this example.

Many firms have implemented the modified method for *all* cases, rather than go through the pre-editing review to determine if 10% is met. This is advisable, when possible. It will enhance the accuracy of the resulting ROR.

While the *day-weighting* formula takes care of one of the problems with *midpoint* methods, it doesn't address the market fluctuation issue. We'll discuss this later.

THE UNIT VALUE METHOD

An alternative approach to measuring performance is the unit value method.[23] This approach is similar to the way mutual fund performance is derived.

A portfolio's starting value is equated to a base value (typically 100 or 1,000). Changes to the portfolio's value due to purchases and sales, market prices, inflows and outflows of cash, corporate actions, etc., are reflected in adjustments to the base value. Performance is then derived by comparing a subsequent period's adjusted base value with the starting base or any intermediate value. Table 2–1 shows a brief example of an application of the unit value approach.

We start by equating the portfolio's market value to a base unit—in this case, 1,000. Knowing the unit value, we can determine the *number of units* in the portfolio by dividing the market value by the unit value:

$$Number\ of\ Units = \frac{Market\ Value}{Unit\ Value}$$

In our case,

$$Number\ of\ Units = \frac{\$550,000}{1,000} = 550$$

The number of units will change only if a cash flow occurs. The unit value, however, will vary as the market value of the portfolio changes. We see this on the second day, when the market value rises from \$500,000 to \$555,000. We now want to derive the *unit value*. This is done by dividing the market value by the number of units:

$$Unit\ Value = \frac{Market\ Value}{Number\ of\ Units} = \frac{\$555,000}{1,000} = 1,009.0909$$

T A B L E   2–1

Day	Market Value	Cash Flow	Number of Units	Unit Value
1	\$550,000	0	550	1,000
2	\$555,000	0	550	1,009.0909
3	\$566,000	+\$10,000	559.9099	1,010.8769
4	\$566,500	0	559.9099	1,011.7699
5	\$561,000	−\$5,000	554.9681	1,010.8689

On Day 3, we have an inflow of $10,000. This means the number of units will increase. We have to determine the number of units $10,000 represents. This is done by dividing the cash value by the prior period's unit value.

$$Number\ of\ Units = \frac{Cash\ Flow}{Prior\ Period's\ Unit\ Value} = \frac{\$10,000}{1,009.0909} = 9.9099$$

The Market Value on Day 3 includes the cash flow, so the revised unit value is based on the updated number of units (reflecting the additional 9.9099 from the $10,000 cash flow).

Day 4 shows a slight increase in the portfolio's market value. The number of units remains unchanged, since no cash flows occurred. The unit value is updated as before.

Finally, on Day 5, we have an outflow of $5,000. We determine the number of units this amount represents based on the prior period's unit value:

$$Number\ of\ Units = \frac{Cash\ Flow}{Prior\ Period's\ Unit\ Value} = \frac{\$5,000}{1,011.7699} = 4.9418$$

This amount is deducted from the prior period's number of units to derive the new value for Day 5. As before, we determine the unit value by dividing the market value by the number of units.

This is essentially the approach used to update the unit value and number of units. Next, we need to see how to calculate performance based on unit values.

From the first day to the fifth, we calculate performance by dividing the ending unit value by the beginning unit value, subtracting 1, and multiplying by 100:

$$Rate\ of\ Return_{1-5} = \left[\left(\frac{Ending\ Unit\ Value}{Beginning\ Unit\ Value}\right) - 1\right] \cdot 100$$

$$= \left[\left(\frac{1,010.8689}{1,000}\right) - 1\right] \cdot 100 = [1.0108689 - 1] \cdot 100 = 1.08689\% = 1.09\%$$

One of the attractions of the unit value method is it easily allows for determination of returns for any period for which the starting and ending unit values are known. For example, we can derive the return from Day 3 to Day 4 simply by using the formula we just employed:

$$Rate\ of\ Return_{3\text{-}4} = \left[\left(\frac{1,011.769}{1,010.8769}\right) - 1\right] \cdot 100 = [(1.0009) - 1] \cdot 100 = 0.9\%$$

To accomplish this, unit values must be maintained for every day in the period. Often, only the month-end unit values are stored, due to the computer storage capacity that would otherwise be required.

A shortcoming with this method arises when an adjustment is needed to a prior period that would affect the number of units. Since the unit value of each subsequent period is dependent on the prior unit values and number of units, such an adjustment would necessitate the revaluation of subsequent period values. For example, if we learned that on Day 3 the inflow was not $10,000 but actually $10,500, we would have to recalculate that day's *number of units* and *unit value*, and the subsequent period's *unit values* and *number of units*. Or, if there was a pricing error, recalculations would be required.

This method presumes that the portfolio's market value is at least repriced whenever cash flows occur.[24] This yields a *true* time-weighted rate of return, rather than the *approximate* returns calculated previously.

GEOMETRIC LINKING

While it's helpful to be able to report a manager's returns for a month or quarter, managers, clients and prospects typically want to see returns for longer periods, e.g., year-to-date, year, multi-year periods, and inception-to-date.

For example, do we derive a quarter's return from three monthly returns? This is done using *geometric linking*.

Let's take an example. During the first quarter, an account had the returns shown in Table 2–2. What's the return for the full quarter?

TABLE 2–2

	Starting Value	Ending Value	Return
January	$1,000	$1,011	1.10%
February	$1,011	$1,018.58	0.75%
March	$1,018.58	$1,032.33	1.35%

TABLE   2–3

Step 1	Divide ROR by 100 (convert percentage into decimal)	1.10 ÷ 100 = 0.0110 0.75 ÷ 100 = 0.0075 1.35 ÷ = 0.0135
Step 2	Add 1	0.0110 + 1 = 1.0110 0.0075 + 1 = 1.0075 0.0135 + 1 = 1.0135
Step 3	Multiply	1.0110 * 1.0075 * 1.0135 = 1.0323
Step 4	Subtract 1	1.0323 – 1 = 0.0323
Step 5	Multiply by 100 (convert decimal into percentage)	0.0323 * 100 = 3.23%

One might be tempted to simply add the three returns together (1.10 + 0.75 + 1.35 = 3.2%). The problem with this is that it doesn't reflect the effect of *compounding* that takes place from one period to the next. We employ *geometric linking* in order to achieve accurate period returns. A five-step process is used to do this (see Table 2–3). The first quarter's return is found to be 3.23 percent.

This same approach is used to link any group of period returns together—days, months, years, etc. For example, a portfolio has the returns shown in Table 2–4 for a 5-year period. The 5-year return is determined using the same approach as above, as shown in Table 2–5. The rate of return for this 5-year period is determined to be 25.68%.

TABLE   2–4

1990	8.52%
1991	6.45%
1992	–2.03%
1993	7.85%
1994	2.97%

TABLE   2–5

Step 1	Divide ROR by 100	$8.52 \div 100 = 0.0852$
	(convert percentage	$6.45 \div 100 = 0.0645$
	into decimal)	$-2.03 \div 100 = 0.0203$
		$7.85 \div 100 = 0.0785$
		$2.97 \div 100 = 0.0297$
Step 2	Add 1	$8.52 + 1 = 1.0852$
		$6.45 + 1 = 1.0645$
		$-2.03 + 1 = 0.9797$
		$7.85 + 1 = 1.0785$
		$2.97 + 1 = 1.0297$
Step 3	Multiply	$1.0852\ *$
		$1.0645\ *$
		$0.9797\ *$
		$1.0785\ *$
		$1.0297 =$
		1.2568
Step 4	Subtract 1	$1.2568 - 1 = 0.2568$
Step 5	Multiply by 100	$0.2568\ *\ 100 = 25.68\%$
	(convert decimal into	
	percentage) year-to	

ANNUALIZED RETURNS

Portfolio managers, clients, and prospects often want to see multi-year returns reflected on an annualized basis. That is, to show the equivalent yearly return for each of the years in the period that would have been needed to derive the overall period return. While we can easily calculate the return for each of the years (or fractional years) in the period, returns will most likely fluctuate from year to year. We want to know what single return would have had to be derived for each of the years in the subperiod to arrive at the overall period return. This process is referred to as *annualization*. It yields *annualized* rates of return.

The 5-year return for the example above is 25.68%. Each year's return varies, from −2.03 to 8.52. What equivalent return would we have had to have for each year to achieve 25.68% for the period?

To determine this, we *don't* divide the 5-year return by 25.68%. This would not take into consideration the compounding that takes place from one year to the next. Instead, we have a formula that brings us the accurate result.

Once again, we use a five-step method (see Table 2–6).

T A B L E   2–6

Step 1	Divide ROR by 100 (convert percentage into decimal)	$25.68 \div = 0.2568$
Step 2	Add 1	$0.2568 + 1 = 1.2568$
Step 3	Take the nth root, where n equals the time period (in this case, 5 years)	$\sqrt[5]{1.2568} = 1.0468$
Step 4	Subtract 1	$1.0468 - 1 = 0.468$
Step 5	Multiply by 100 (convert decimal into percentage)	$0.468 * 100 = 4.68\%$

(Please note that an alternative to calculating the nth root in Step 3 above is to raise the value from step 2 to the inverse of the number of years' power. E.g., instead of finding the 5th root of 1.02568, raise 1.02568 to the 1/5th power. This is an equivalent mathematical function that yields the same result.)

The *annualized* return for this 5-year period is 4.68%. The 25.68% return could have been achieved had we had annual returns of 4.68% for each of the 5 years in the period. We can prove this by *geometrically linking* 5-year returns of 4.68% (see Table 2–7). The two-basis-point difference (25.68 vs. 25.70) is due to rounding.

You may encounter a situation where you're dealing with a period of years that includes a fractional year. How is the annualized rate of return determined for such a time frame? It's done by using the exact same method.

This situation often arises when we're calculating a client's *inception-to-date* return. Your client's rate of return for a 27-month period is 33.17%. What's the annualized ROR for this period? Using the previously discussed formula, we would do the calculations shown in Table 2–8.

Using this formula, we were able to determine that the annualized ROR for this 2.25 year period is 13.58%.

Industry Rule: Don't annualize for periods less than one year. Mathematically, we can take a 3-month return and extrapolate an annual return. However, the *industry standard* practice is *not* to annualize a return if the period is less than a year. To do so would be incorrect, since the period is much too short to attempt to derive a return for a year from it.

T A B L E   2–7

Step 1	Divide ROR by 100 (convert percentage into decimal)	4.68 ÷ 100 = 0.0468
		4.68 ÷ 100 = 0.0468
		4.68 ÷ 100 = 0.0468
		4.68 ÷ 100 = 0.0468
		4.68 ÷ 100 = 0.0468
Step 2	Add 1	0.0468 + 1 = 1.0468
		0.0468 + 1 = 1.0468
		0.0468 + 1 = 1.0468
		0.0468 + 1 = 1.0468
		0.0468 + 1 = 1.0468
Step 3	Multiply	1.0468 *
		1.0468 *
		1.0468 *
		1.0468 *
		1.0468 =
		1.2570
Step 4	Subtract 1	1.2570 – 1 = 0.2570
Step 5	Multiply by 100 (convert decimal into percentage)	0.2570 * 100 = 25.70%

For example, a manager might have a couple of very good months when her returns are very high, but to expect to have a similar success over a complete year is considered ambitious, and to attempt to report such a number would be misleading.

T A B L E   2–8

Step 1	Divide ROR by 100 (convert percentage into decimal)	33.17 ÷ 100 = 0.3317
Step 2	Add 1	0.3317 + 1 = 1.3317
Step 3	Take the *nth* root, where *n* equals the time period (in this case, 27 months equals 2.25 years)	$\sqrt[2.25]{1.3317} = 1.1358$
Step 4	Subtract 1	1.1358 – 1 + 0.1358
Step 5	Multiply by 100 (convert decimal into percentage)	0.1358 * 100 = 13.58%

MUTUAL FUND PERFORMANCE

The U.S. mutual fund industry must report rates of return in compliance with the rules of the Securities and Exchange Commission.

Unlike private account money management, which typically caters to high-net-worth individuals or institutional investors, the mutual fund industry's typical accounts are retail—often involving less-sophisticated investors. The SEC is conscious of this and has established a variety of regulations governing the reporting and advertising of performance information. The concern is that some investors could be taken advantage of by misleading information.

The SEC has not established rules regarding the calculation of rates of return for private accounts. They have, however, defined the appropriate way to calculate mutual fund returns. Appendix E provides detailed information on these calculations.

TECHNOLOGY'S ROLE

It's not coincidental that the expansion of performance measurement's methods and complexity (and the related topics we'll discuss later) has happened at the same time we've seen tremendous improvements in technology. The reality is that we would not be where we are today without the advantages technology brings us. One wonders whether technology was the horse pulling the performance measurement cart. As noted earlier, the IRR formula was developed because so many investment firms had no access to a computer. They were simply out of the reach of most money managers. The PC revolution has changed that. Calculation horsepower has been significantly enhanced by the price/performance advances in computer technology, especially in personal computers.

The technological advances also allow for improvements in the accuracy, regularity, and availability of security prices, permitting more accurate and timely pricing of securities. Thus, there's greater comfort in the valuation of client holdings. Technology also permits the automation of reconciliation between the adviser and the client's custodian, thus adding even greater accuracy to the performance measurement process.

Inexpensive laser and color printers have allowed firms to enhance their presentation of information. Powerful, inexpensive software programs permit information to be presented in graphical formats, thus enhancing the communication of information.

The reality is that there would not be this level of interest or capability without the technology that's available today. Many of the things we'll discuss later in this book would not exist, including style analysis, performance attribution, or the AIMR standards. Without technology, they probably wouldn't even be concepts. Technology has permitted what used to be a very limited presentation to expand and grow, in information content and flexibility.

CHAPTER SUMMARY

We've introduced several concepts in this chapter. Several formulas were introduced to calculate *time-weighted* rates of return, as opposed to *dollar-weighted* rates of return. They included the ICAA method, the Dietz midpoint formula, the Dietz day-weighted formula, and the unit value method.

We demonstrated how subperiod (e.g., monthly) returns can be *geometrically linked* to derive longer period (e.g., quarter, year, multiyear) returns. We showed how to calculate the *annualized* rate of return for a multiyear period. We also talked briefly about the role of technology, and how it has permitted the growth of the performance measurement and reporting function.

These formulas and concepts are the basis for deriving rates of return. The next chapter will build on this base of knowledge.

ENDNOTES

1. BAI [1968], p. 15.
2. Continuous compounding contrasts with discrete compounding. Discrete compounding describes the use of certain time periods (e.g., monthly, quarterly, semiannually, annually) when income or appreciation is realized. Continuous compounding occurs continuously over the time period.
3. The preferred approach for this simple example would be to *geometrically link* (to be discussed later on) the two periods' returns (10% and 40%) to derive the return for the full period, and then annualize the results. Doing this, we get a two-year period return of 54% and an annualized ROR of 24.1%, regardless of the cash flows. This is clearly preferable to the dollar-weighted returns, which are impacted by the cash flows.
4. We could have an account that's established with a starting value of zero. The initial contribution would be a cash flow. Depending on the return formula, treating this as a cash flow could have unpredictable results. Consequently, we normally treat the initial "flow" as the starting position.

5. "Tax basis" is a term that's applicable to taxable accounts. It refers to the acquisition value of an asset. It's relevant when the asset is sold. The profit or loss from the sale transaction will be computed by comparing the tax basis value with the sales value.

6. For example, interest paid by municipal bonds is often nontaxable, while interest paid by corporate bonds is usually taxable.

7. *Paper* profits or losses refer to what your portfolio looks like on paper—that is, the value of an asset as priced by the market, but for which cash hasn't been generated. You don't pay tax on *paper* profits, only *realized,* actual profits in which cash was generated.

8. Williams [1988].

9. *Linking* or *geometric linking* is taken up later in this chapter.

10. ICAA [1971], p. 24.

11. By "independent" I mean those advisers that weren't affiliates or subsidiaries of banks, insurance companies, or brokerage firms.

12. ICAA [1971], p. 7.

13. As we'll discuss later, it isn't clear that a time-weighted ROR is necessarily appropriate for subportfolio returns.

14. Even today, many firms value their portfolios less frequently than daily.

15. We will discuss the return differences between *approximate* and *true* time-weighted returns later in chapter 3.

16. Kirschman and Dietz [1983].

17. The ICAA method also reflects reinvested income in the beginning and ending market values.

18. In the piece by Dietz and Kirschman, the issues of cash flows and pricing were addressed: "It is generally agreed that more frequent measurement periods (shorter time intervals) result in more accurate returns … However, as a practical matter trustee/custodian banks and investment management firms usually do not have systems in place that allow for valuation more frequently than monthly, nor has there been a great demand for such services from institutional investors." The situation has obviously changed since this piece was written, since monthly or quarterly pricing is less common except for the most difficult to price securities. While there are still a number of firms that value portfolios monthly, the trend is definitely towards daily pricing.

19. A basis point is 1/100th of a percentage point.

20. While this 10% rule seems to have been universally accepted, some firms use a lower threshold to improve on accuracy.

21. Ideally, the firm should revalue the portfolio on days when large flows occur. The next chapter takes up the concept of daily valuations and increasing the accuracy even further.

22. For example, if on the 15th we received a contribution of $10,000 and also distributed $9,950, our net cash flow for the day would be $50.

23. The earliest reference the author could find to this topic is [Sieff 1966] pp. 93–99.

24. Actually, the day before and the day of the cash flow, since the number of units the flow equates to will be based on the prior day's unit value. That value will be correct only if it's based on an accurately priced portfolio.

CHAPTER 3

Other ROR Issues

In this chapter, we'll be discussing several other topics relating to calculating rates of return, including methods of enhancing the accuracy of the return, handling income accruals, deriving subportfolio returns, and allocation of cash.

IMPROVING THE ACCURACY

As discussed in chapter 2, the *approximation* methods assume that all flows occur in the middle of the measurement period. This assumption is faulty for two reasons. First, flows can occur at any time in the period. By assuming midmonth, we will often be either overstating or understating the amount of time the money coming in or going out was actually being managed. Secondly, the market can fluctuate quite a bit. The assumption that the market moves linearly from the beginning to the end of the month is typically incorrect.

Steve Lerit discussed this very issue of the impact of cash flows and market volatility on rates of return calculations.[1] The effect of cash flows by themselves varied depending on their magnitude. The larger the flow, the greater the error. When large flows occur during periods of market volatility, the error increases significantly. In his article, Lerit demonstrated where an error of almost a full percentage point could occur. This may not seem like much, but it is, especially in a competitive environment. In reality, even greater errors could take place if the volatility is quite significant.

Given how the security markets have become more volatile since the early 1980s, the justification for moving toward the more accurate *true* time-weighted rates of return is becoming clearer. Also, the availability of daily security pricing for most securities makes undertaking this method more feasible. And finally, packaged software exists to provide the necessary functionality for daily rates of return.

ACHIEVING ENHANCED ACCURACY

The modified Dietz method is still an *approximation* formula. The one flaw in this method is the *assumption* that the portfolio's market value progresses linearly from the beginning of the month to the end (see Figure 3–1). The reality is that a portfolio's market price can vary considerably through a month, as shown in Figure 3–2.

F I G U R E   3–1

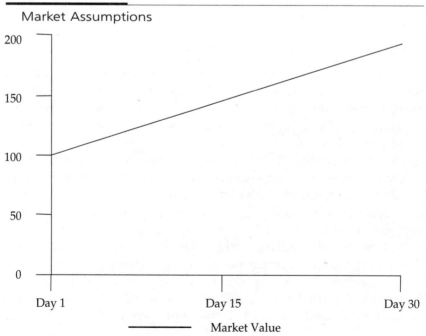

Market Assumptions

——————— Market Value

F I G U R E   3–2

Market Realities

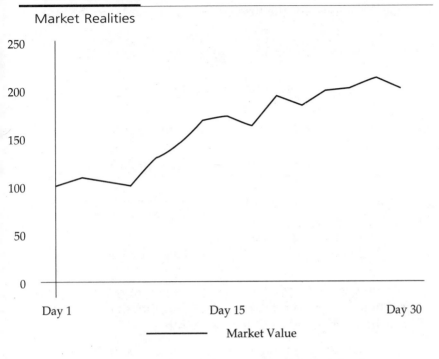

Market Value

To overcome the shortcomings of the *modified* method, we can use a *daily valuation* method. In this approach, the portfolio is valued *daily*, or at least whenever cash flows occur.[2] Rates of return are calculated daily and *geometrically linked*[3] together to arrive at the period's ROR.

Here's an example. An account starts the month with $1,000. On the 5th, $100 is added. Then on the 12th, another $100 is added. Let's calculate the ROR:

Beginning of Month
   Market Value = $1,000

5th of Month
   Value of Account *before* cash flow = $1,010[4]
   Value of Account *after* cash flow = $1,110

12th of Month
   Value of Account *before* cash flow = $1,115
   Value of Account *after* cash flow = $1,215

End of Month
   Value of Account = $1,230

Using the simple formula we introduced in chapter 1, we first calculate the return for the first period (from the 1st to the 5th):

$$ROR_{1-5} = \left[\left(\frac{EMV - BMV}{BMV} \right) \right] \cdot 100$$

$$= \frac{(1{,}010 - 1{,}000)}{1{,}000} = 0.01 \text{ or } 1\%$$

Next, we calculate the return for the *next* subperiod.

$$ROR_{5-12} = \frac{(1{,}115 - 1{,}110)}{1{,}110} = .0045 \text{ or } 0.45\%$$

Finally, we calculate the return from the 12th through the end of the month:

$$ROR_{12-30} = \frac{(1{,}230 - 1{,}215)}{1{,}215} = 0.0122 \text{ or } 1.22\%$$

We now *geometrically link* these three period returns to derive the *true* time-weighted rate of return for the month (see Table 3–1). The *true* time-weighted ROR for the month is 2.69%. To recap:

- Break the period into subperiods, bounded by cash flows.
- Calculate the portfolio's market value at each cash flow, specifying the value *before* and *after* the flow.

T A B L E   3–1

Step 1	Divide ROR by 100 (convert percentage into decimal)	1% ÷ 100 = 0.0100 0.45% ÷ 100 = 0.0045 1.22% ÷ 100 = 0.0122
Step 2	Add 1	0.0100 + 1 = 1.0100 0.0045 + 1 = 1.0045
0.0122 + 1 = 1.0122		
Step 3	Multiply	1.0100 * 1.0045 * 1.0122 = 1.0269
Step 4	Subtract 1	1.0269 − 1 = 0.0269
Step 5	Multiply by 100 (convert decimal into percentage)	0.0269 * 100 = 2.69%

- Calculate the returns for each subperiod.
- Geometrically link the subperiod returns to derive the return for the period.

SHORTCOMINGS OF TRUE TIME-WEIGHTED RETURNS

Although a true time-weighted return, or daily ROR, is normally highly desirable, there are a few shortcomings. First, to derive accurate returns using this method, portfolios must be priced on a daily basis[5] and these prices must be accurate. This may not always be possible, since accurate prices may not always be attainable for certain securities during the month (e.g., private placements, international, and certain fixed-income securities). However, prices for many, if not most, securities should be available on a daily basis. Pricing should also be synchronized with corporate actions (e.g., stock splits, spinoffs, reorganizations).

A second, related, issue is the need for accurate account information regarding positions. For example, all corporate actions (e.g., stock splits, distributions) should be processed, all income received should be recorded, and cash positions must be verified as correct.

Investment firms typically undergo a monthly reconciliation[6] with client custodians in order to ensure that their view of the client portfolios is accurate. On occasion, adjustments must be made to client accounts. A daily ROR would require a high level of confidence in the accuracy of information. In the event a monthly reconciliation reveals a discrepancy, adjustments would be needed to prior days, resulting in corrected RORs. When adjustments are made, returns should be recalculated to ensure their accuracy.

Third, a daily rate of return system requires a computer system that is flexible enough to provide the necessary calculations, reporting, and adjustments. This isn't always the case, though more and more portfolio accounting systems are adding these features. Also, several software vendors have performance measurement systems that provide these capabilities.

Any firm that wants to have daily rates of return should ensure that their system supports prior period adjustments. How far back the system can go (e.g., up to a month, up to three months, indefinitely) should be taken into consideration. However, allowing prior period adjustments too far back could impact the overall integrity of the performance measurement system.

ADVANTAGES OF TRUE TIME-WEIGHTED RETURNS

The most obvious advantage of true time-weighted ROR is the higher accuracy in reporting. A volatile market and large cash flows can cause an *approximation* method to be less accurate.

In addition, a firm that undertakes this step will have increased reporting capabilities. For example, a portfolio manager can see daily returns rather than only monthly returns. Normally, this isn't necessary. However, when there are large shifts in the market, managers often want to know the resulting impact on their clients' portfolios. Without a daily ROR system, this is difficult if not impossible. Reporting can also be done for odd periods within the month (month-to-date, current-week-to-date, prior week). Such reporting can prove helpful.

Firms can also respond to client requests for up-to-date reporting of performance. Requests for such information often come in when large shifts occur in the market. More and more, firms are finding themselves in the position where their clients want up-to-date returns. If a firm isn't able to respond to such requests, clients become curious about the degree of sophistication in the firm's computer processing area.

ACCRUING FOR INCOME

Income accrues[7] over a period of time. This is especially true for fixed-income securities that make periodic (e.g., semiannual) interest payments. Each day between pay dates, the interest that is owed will increase until the interest payment is made. Since the bond holder is entitled to this interest amount, his holding's true market value should reflect this amount. The value of a fixed-income security at a purchase or sale almost always includes accrued interest.

As a general practice, performance should be based on accruals. Intuitively, it isn't obvious why this should be done. After all, one might argue that recognizing the interest when it is received will more than make up for the lack of accruals during the intervening period. However, this isn't the reality in practice.

The simple example in Table 3–2 shows how performance can be impacted if accruals aren't taken into consideration.

In this example, we've purchased a bond and paid the amount that had accrued (two months' worth) to the prior owner, since we will receive this amount when the bond issuer makes payment in four months. The fact that the bond's market value hasn't fluctuated during this period has no impact on the results, since any appreciation or depreciation would be felt in a similar manner by either approach.

Can you imagine the client's reaction when she learns that the $100,000 she gave you to invest is now only worth $99,000 after

T A B L E   3–2

	Accrual	Cash
Starting position—first quarter	$100,000	$100,000
Initial transaction: buy 6% bond with 2 months' accrued interest		
Principal amount of transaction	$99,000	$99,000
Accrued interest paid (2 months)	$1,000	$1,000
Ending position		
Bond's market value	$99,000	$99,000
Accrued interest (5 months)	$2,500	-0-
Total market value	$101,500	$99,000
Ending period return (end of first quarter)	1.5%	–1%
Starting position—second quarter	$101,500	$99,000
Ending position		
Bond's market value	$99,000	$99,000
Cash (from bond interest payment)	$3,000	$3,000
Accrued interest (2 months)	$1,000	-0-
Ending period return (end of second quarter)	1.5%	3%
Two-quarter return	3%	2%

only 3 months of management? The interesting thing is that most firms *will* include the accrual amount on their position summary, since the client is entitled to this amount. But traditionally, many firms *didn't* include the accrual in the calculation, believing that it would *work itself out* in the long term.

As our example shows, this isn't the case. In this case, the manager is underreporting performance if he fails to include the accrual in the calculation. There may be cases when the failure to accrue interest will result in an overstatement of performance.

With today's systems and the availability of information, interest accruals should be a standard part of performance.

ACCRUAL OF DIVIDENDS

Many firms want to accrue for their equities that pay dividends. This is acceptable as long as the timing is right. Just because a company paid a dividend in the past is no guarantee they'll pay one in the future, or that the amount of the dividend will equal the prior amount. To accrue (as we do for bonds) during the intervening period between dividend payments would therefore be incorrect. Also, unlike bonds, the owner isn't entitled to payment of the dividend when the security is sold *unless* the sale takes place after the record date.

To properly accrue for equities, the dividend amount can be (and probably should be) reflected in the asset's value after ex-date. In general, the benefit of accruing for dividends is insignificant. However, if the yield (dividend ÷ price) of a dividend-paying security is relatively large, the price of the security can fluctuate significantly between the time before and after ex-date, thus giving even more reason for accruing dividends.

CALCULATING SUBPORTFOLIO LEVEL RETURNS

There's an increasing demand for the reporting of performance below the portfolio level. This is partly an attribution issue, but there are other reasons as well.

When two or more managers have responsibility for a client's account, the firm may wish to see how each individual manager performed; how each contributed to the client's overall performance. So, performance will be calculated on the basis of the assets each manager was responsible for—typically divided by asset type (fixed-income manager versus equity manager).

Clients often want to see their performance broken up by industry or security type. This gives them an appreciation for the way each sector performed, and how this performance will vary over time. A manager may want to validate a particular strategy she's employed, and the best way to do this might be to split out those securities that represent that strategy and measure their performance.

The typical levels of interest include asset class or segment, (equity, fixed-income), industry sector, and security. In order to calculate *any* level below portfolio, the securities must carry an identifier in the portfolio accounting system that points to the particular group. These identifiers or codes are typically established on the security master file. These codes can include security type and industry group. Other tables within a firm's portfolio accounting system may group security types and industry group codes into other categories (see Table 3–3). There are a variety of ways to calculate a subportfolio return. We'll discuss three.

Method 1—Using an Approximation Method

The first method deals with the situation where we don't calculate daily rates of return, nor do we maintain daily market values. Consequently, we'll rely on the beginning and ending market values, plus the cash flows that take place during the month, to derive the sector's performance. Our starting balance will be the value of the stocks in the portfolio.

T A B L E   3–3

Typical Identifier Fields for Security File
- Security type (corporate bond, municipal bond, common stock, preferred stock, option, mutual fund)
- Industry code (SIC codes are often used)
- Sector (automotive, oil & gas, telecommunications)
- Segment (stocks, bonds)

One convention that's often used to derive subportfolio rates of return is to treat all buy and sell transactions as cash flows. A *buy* will be treated as an *inflow*, since cash has to come into the sector to make the purchase. A *sell* is treated as an *outflow*, because cash has been generated as a result of the sale and it's not being maintained in a sector-cash bucket, so we're releasing it to the general overall cash bucket. Table 3–4 reflects the portfolio holdings at the beginning of the month.

On the 10th of the month, the equity manager sells Stock A for $6,500 and purchases Stock C for $5,000. No other equity transactions are done between the 10th and the end of the month, so we have the ending position shown in Table 3–5. We'll use the *day-weighted Dietz formula* we introduced earlier:

$$R = \left(\frac{EMV - (1 - WD) \cdot C}{BMV + (WD \cdot C)} - 1 \right) \cdot 100$$

We don't keep track of daily market values, but instead will compare the beginning period value with the ending, and take into consideration any transactions that occurred that impact the equity sector. As noted above, the portfolio manager sold Stock A for $6,500, so this will be treated as an outflow. He also purchased Stock C for $5,000. This will be treated as an inflow.

We need to calculate the "WD" values in the Dietz formula to day-weight the cash flows. The WD factor is calculated as follows:

$$WD = \frac{CD - D}{CD} = \frac{30 - 10}{30} = \frac{20}{30} = \frac{2}{3}$$

T A B L E   3–4

Beginning Period Holdings

Security	Market Value
Stock A	$5,000
Stock B	$5,000
Bond D	$5,000
Bond E	$5,000
Cash	$2,000

T A B L E   3–5

Ending Period Holdings

Stock A	$5,000
Stock B	$5,000
Stock C	$5,000
Bond D	$5,250
Bond E	$5,000
Cash	$3,512

where

CD = number of calendar days in the period (30)
D = the day the cash flow occurred (15th)

This fraction reflects the amount of time during the month in which the *inflow* was in the portfolio or the *outflow* was out of the portfolio. Since the flows occurred on the 10th, there were 20 days in the month when the flows were in/out. This represents two-thirds of the month.

We now calculate the ROR for this month:

$$R = \left[\frac{10,000 - (1 - \frac{2}{3}) \cdot (-6500 + 5000)}{10,000 + \frac{2}{3} \cdot (-6500 + 5000)} - 1 \right] \cdot 100$$

$$= \left[\frac{10,000 - \frac{1}{3} \cdot (-1500)}{10,000 + \frac{2}{3} \cdot (-1500)} - 1 \right] \cdot 100$$

$$= \left[\frac{10,000 + 500 - 1}{10,000 - 1000} \right] \cdot 100 = \left[\frac{10,500 - 1}{9,000} \right] \cdot 100 = [1.1667 - 1] \cdot 100 = 16.67\%$$

The return for the equity sector (without cash) is 16.67%.

Method 2—Daily Rates of Return

Now we'll show how we would derive the return using the *true time-weighted rate of return* or *daily rate of return*. As noted earlier, we do not need to show every day's market values, just the day when flows occurred.[8] Above, we showed the beginning and ending period values; Tables 3–6 and 3–7 show the values on the 10th of the month, when the sale and purchase took place.

Please note that in addition to Stock A appreciating in value, Stock B also went up (from a starting value of $5,000 to $5,300). You'll see in a moment how this will affect the overall return.

We'll calculate two returns: the return from the beginning of the month till the 10th, and then from the 10th through the end of the month. We'll use the daily rate of return formula we introduced earlier.

$$ROR_{1-10} = \left[\left(\frac{EMV - BVM}{BMV}\right)\right] \cdot 100$$

$$= \left[\left(\frac{11,800 - 10,000}{10,000}\right)\right] \cdot 100 = \left[\frac{1,800}{10,000}\right] \cdot 100 = 0.18 \cdot 100 = 18\%$$

The return for the first part of the month is 18%. Now, using the same formula, we'll derive the formula for the second part of the month:

$$ROR_{10-30} = \left[\frac{(10,000 - 10,300)}{10,300}\right] \cdot 100 = \left[\frac{-300}{10,300}\right] \cdot 100$$

$$= -0.0291 \cdot 100 = -2.91\%$$

The return for the second part of the month is –2.91%. We can now calculate the return for the month by geometrically linking

T A B L E   3–6

Day 10—Before Transactions

Security	Market Value
Stock A	$6,500
Stock B	$5,300
Bond D	$5,250
Bond E	$5,000
Cash	$2,003

T A B L E   3–7

Day 10—After Transactions

Security	Market Value
Stock B	$5,000
Stock C	$5,300
Bond D	$5,250
Bond E	$5,000
Cash	$3,503

these two returns. Doing this, we determine that the monthly return is 14.57%. Why the difference with the approximate method?

The approximate method only took into consideration the beginning and ending market values, so we were unaware that Stock B had appreciated during the first part of the month. It consequently dropped in value for the second part of the month, resulting in a negative return (the equity sector went from $11,300 to $11,000).

Cash Allocation

The first two methods didn't account for cash. They were *sector only* returns. Since a manager often has a portion of the cash allocated to him, any return on cash should be reflected in his return. Before we discuss how to measure performance by allocating cash, we'll discuss cash allocation.

There is a variety of ways to allocate cash, but three general rules that should be applied:

1. The method should be decided on *before* the end of the period. Otherwise, *games* could be played in an attempt to enhance sector returns.

2. The method should be applied consistently. Firms shouldn't be switching allocation rules unless there's a clear justification.

3. The method chosen shouldn't be arbitrary. It should be reasonable and fair.

What do I mean by not being arbitrary. Well, I'll give you an example of a cash allocation rule I consider arbitrary. Hopefully, it will convey my meaning.

Here's a method I've seen employed:

$$Equity\ Cash\ Percentage = \frac{Market\ Value\ of\ Equities}{Total\ Amount\ Invested}$$

$$Bond\ Cash\ Percentage = \frac{Market\ Value\ of\ Bonds}{Total\ Amount\ Invested}$$

Why is this arbitrary? A firm that claims to be a "balanced manager" should be making *asset allocation* decisions, that is, designating the amount of the entire portfolio that is to be invested in stocks and the amount to be invested in bonds.[9] Cash would therefore be *earmarked* for each asset type. At the end of a period, one manager may be *fully invested* while another may have cash that's still left to be invested. To apply a rule like this would cause the fully invested manager to take on some of the cash return, when in reality none of that cash is hers to be invested. Consequently, any allocation rule that's applied should be somewhat sensitive to the overall asset allocation strategy. Now we'll briefly discuss three methods of cash allocation.

Separate Cash Buckets

The most accurate way of tracking cash is to have separate "buckets" for each sector's cash. Cash for any purchases for that sector would come from that sector's bucket. Sales would cause cash to be moved into that bucket. Any income that's derived from that sector's investments would go into that sector's bucket. If a decision is made to alter the asset allocation percentages, cash would be moved from one sector's bucket into the other.

Although this is the most accurate cash allocation method, it's also the most difficult to apply. Most portfolio accounting systems do not support it.

Separate Portfolios

This approach is similar to the first. Here, individual portfolios (or subportfolios) will be established for each asset type. This is equivalent to having separate cash buckets.

The challenge is that these portfolios are *pseudo* accounts. The custodian only knows a single account, but the manager has two or more (to represent each of the asset classes). Income needs to be allocated across the subportfolios by the accounting system. This approach is often easier to implement than the former.

Tie Back to Asset Allocation Percentages

Balanced managers establish target percentages for each asset class. For example,

$$\text{Equities} = 60\%$$
$$\text{Fixed income} = 35\%$$
$$\text{Cash} = 5\%$$

To *tie back* the ending-period cash to the asset allocation percentages, we compare the *actual* amount invested with the *targets*. Then we'd adjust the cash to arrive at the targets (see Table 3–8).

Now I'll demonstrate how we would derive the sector-plus return using this example. As you can see, both the stock and bond sectors are underinvested. The returns are derived as follows:

$$ROR_{stock\ plus\ cash} =$$

$$\frac{Market\ Value\ of\ Equities}{Equity\ Target} \cdot ROR_{stock} + \frac{Market\ Value\ of\ Cash}{Equity\ Target} \cdot ROR_{cash}$$

$$= \frac{55,000}{60,000} \cdot 18\% + \frac{5,000}{60,000} \cdot 2\% = 16.5\% + 0.17\% = 16.67\%$$

T A B L E   3–8

Sector	ROR	Amount Invested		Target		Amount of Cash Needed to Meet Target
Stocks	18%	$55,000	55%	$60,000	60%	$5,000
Bonds	9%	$34,000	34%	$35,000	35%	$1,000
Cash	2%	$11,000	11%	$5,000	5%	–$6,000

$$ROR_{bonds\ plus\ cash} =$$

$$\frac{Market\ Value\ of\ Bonds}{Bond\ Target} \cdot ROR_{bonds} + \frac{Market\ Value\ of\ Cash \cdot ROR_{cash}}{Bond\ Target}$$

$$= \frac{34,000}{35,000} \cdot 9\% + \frac{1,000}{35,000} \cdot 2\% = 8.74\% + 0.06\% = 8.80\%$$

There are variations on this approach. For example, what if one manager is overinvested, thus depriving the other manager of cash? Some firms will *penalize* the manager who's overinvested by deducting a *loan fee*. In other cases, the manager won't be penalized, but the underinvested manager won't be penalized either, since the cash wasn't available to be invested. Instead, they'll simply get all the cash return.

Predefined Allocation Percentage
Another method that can be used is to define what the ending allocation will be *before* the end of the period. For example, the firm may simply state that at the end of this month, 35% of the residual cash will go to the bond manager, and 65% to the equity manager. Often, this percentage will simply be the asset allocation percentage. While many find this method acceptable, I feel it borders on being arbitrary, and therefore don't recommend it.

Method 3—Allocation of Cash

Now, we'll calculate the returns of the sectors *without* cash, and then allocate a portion of the cash return to the sector returns. We derived the stock-only return earlier, using both the approximation and true time-weighted return methods. For this example, we'll use the approximation method's result, which was 16.67%.

Now, we'll calculate the return for the cash sector, again using the approximation method. On the 10th of the month, two transactions occurred (a sale of Stock A for $6,500 and a purchase of Stock C for $5,000). This resulted in a net inflow of $1,500 into cash. This was the only cash flow for the month.

We also received income, which we'll assume to have been 100% derived from the cash investment.[10] The return is derived as follows:

$$R = \frac{\left[3{,}512 - \left(1 - \frac{2}{3}\right) \cdot (1{,}500) - 1\right] \cdot 100}{\dfrac{2{,}000 + 2 \cdot (1{,}500)}{3}} = \frac{\left[3{,}512 - \frac{1}{3} \cdot (-1{,}500) - 1\right] \cdot 100}{\dfrac{2{,}000 + 2 \cdot (-1{,}500)}{3}}$$

$$= \left[\frac{3{,}512 - 500 - 1}{2{,}000 + 1{,}000}\right] \cdot 100 = \left[\frac{3{,}012 - 1}{3{,}000}\right] \cdot 100 = [1.004 - 1] \cdot 100 = 0.4\%$$

The cash return for the period is 0.4%.

Now we have to combine the cash return with the equity return to derive the *equity-plus-cash* return. We need an *allocation* method.

As discussed above, there is a variety of ways to allocate cash. To simplify this example, we'll use a predetermined percentage based on the asset allocation guidelines—in this case, 50%. This means that 50% of the ending cash is to be assigned to the equity manager.[11]

The ending month market value of stocks is $10,000. We add to this half the ending cash ($3,512 ÷ 2 = $1,756) and come up with the equity-plus-cash market value of $11,756. We can now derive the rate of return as follows:

$$ROR_{equities\ plus\ cash} =$$

$$\frac{MV_{equities}}{Equities\ Plus\ Cash} \cdot ROR_{equities} + \frac{MV_{cash}}{Equities\ Plus\ Cash} \cdot ROR_{cash}$$

$$= \frac{10{,}000}{11{,}756} \cdot 16.67\% + \frac{1{,}756}{11{,}756} \cdot 0.4\% = 14.18\% + 0.01\% = 14.19\%$$

Our equity-plus-cash return is determined to be 14.19%.

COMPARING THE METHODS

We've seen three ways to calculate a subportfolio return, as summarized in Table 3–9.

Our results vary considerably. The first thing to remember is that the first two methods measured the return for the equity sector only. Method 3 allocated cash by using the approximation method. We could have applied cash using the true time-weighted return method, and the result would have been still different.

T A B L E   3–9

Method 1—Approximation	16.67%
Method 2—True Time-Weighted ROR	14.57%
Method 3—Cash Allocation	14.19%

Hopefully, the reader will see that each method can yield different results. Although the improvement in accuracy may not always result in an increase in return, it should yield better numbers. Also, the need to include cash is becoming universally accepted, although the reporting of sector-only returns is also considered valuable.

HOW OFTEN SHOULD WE REPORT PERFORMANCE?

At one time, it was typical for managers to provide clients with rates of return annually. That is, once a year, they would tell their clients how well they (the managers) did in investing the clients' money during the prior year. Often, only one figure (that year's rate of return) was provided.

Today, it's more common for managers to report more frequently and for multiple time periods. For example, some managers report rates of returns for the following time periods:

Monthly

Quarterly

Annually

Five-Year

Ten-Year

Since Inception.[12]

Some clients want to see rolling period[13] returns. For example, returns for a *rolling year*, where the year is not fixed by the calendar. If we were going to report the returns for the end of March, we might show the following:

January

February

March

First Quarter

Rolling 1-Year

(End of March from prior year to end of March for current year)

Since Inception

The additional reporting frequency and time frames are also beneficial for the firm's management. It provides greater insight into how their investment strategies are performing, and how their accounts are doing relative to benchmarks and to each other. During periods of high market volatility, the ability to report in such flexible ways permits managers to better track their portfolios and to make adjustments as necessary.

Performance is also typically reported at the asset class level. Other subportfolio level returns (e.g., by industry) are becoming more common.

Comparison with benchmarks (see chapter 10) is often part of the client's performance reporting package. In addition, charts and graphs are often used to graphically depict performance. And there's an increasing use of color and shape to enhance the presentation.

CHAPTER SUMMARY

In this chapter, we explained the advantages of a daily or *true* time-weighted rate of return. We demonstrated a method for deriving such returns. Although the calculation of daily rates of return has not yet become an industry standard, it's now more common, since firms recognize the advantages of improved accuracy. Also, computer systems that support such an approach are more prevalent.

We provided three methods of calculating rates of return below the portfolio level, two where the return for the asset class without cash was calculated, and a third when we included cash. Three methods of cash allocation were shown, and the shortcomings of others were briefly discussed.

Finally, we touched on how performance reporting has evolved.

ENDNOTES

1. Lerit [1996].
2. Appendix D shows why we only need to value portfolios on the day of cash flows in order to calculate the true time-weighted rate of return.
3. Geometric linking is discussed in chapter 2.
4. The reader may wonder where the additional $10 came from in the market value. This reflects appreciation in the value of the securities. Similar changes in market value will be reflected for the other dates in this example.
5. It's true that portfolios must be accurately priced *whenever* a rate of return is calculated. Many firms don't price all their securities on a daily basis—for example, they may price fixed-income securities on a weekly or monthly basis. In order to have accurate RORs, the market value (which is made up of priced securities) must be accurate.
6. Please refer to the Glossary for a brief explanation of account reconciliation.
7. Please see the Glossary for a brief explanation of accruals.
8. Please refer to Appendix D for an explanation.
9. The reader may have noticed that I'm referring only to bonds and stocks. This is not being done to slight investors in real estate, precious metals, or any other type of asset. Rather, it's being done for simplicity. For the most part, the same guidelines would apply regardless of the asset type.
10. It serves little purpose to overcomplicate this example by discussing the handling of income from the stocks (dividends) or bonds (interest). In reality, income may come from either or both these sectors. The level of precision the firm wants to employ will determine how the income will be handled. Often, one can try to be overly precise, resulting in a lot of work for a negligible improvement in accuracy. Again, the firm can review the potential gain from tracking every dollar of income to determine if this extra effort is justified. Our example is the simplest case. The author will leave it to the reader to explore a more complicated scenario.
11. The author apologizes for being overly simplistic. However, again, little will be gained by making this example more complicated than it needs be. I've demonstrated the way one would allocate cash based on making adjustments to arrive at the asset allocation guidelines. Although I prefer this method when separate buckets aren't being maintained, to repeat the example here would result in a longer discourse, which would serve little purpose. I hope the reader agrees.
12. Since the account's inception or the beginning of the reporting of performance. Often, an agreement will be reached between the client and the manager that the reporting of performance will commence at some date following the initial transfer of funds, to allow the manager time to establish the initial investments.
13. A *rolling period* is one that isn't fixed as we normally think of it with a calendar. For example, a calendar year goes from January to December, but a rolling year would be a 12-month period that moves through the year—for example, we might start with January to December, then February to January, then March to February, and so on.

CHAPTER 4

Performance Attribution

By itself, knowing a manager's return is becoming less important. Performance attribution is an attempt to determine the cause(s) or source(s) for the return. There can be many different factors that can contribute to the resulting return, and managers and their clients want to know what the source is, or how each factor contributed (or detracted from) the return. Managers are also interested in attribution because it can help validate their investment process. This chapter will provide a basic introduction to the concept of performance attribution.

SIMPLE EXAMPLE—GOOD OR BAD MANAGER?

Here's a simple example: A manager's performance is reported as 15%. The comparison benchmark for this period is 13%. At first glance, we might conclude that the manager did a good job. But let's take a closer look at the portfolio's holdings (see Table 4–1). Did this manager perform well? Is he a good or bad manager? Would you hire him after seeing this information?

The portfolio is comprised of ten securities, nine of which had average returns of only 1%. The manager picked one big winner, which yielded a return of 141%. Was this luck or skill? Given the manager's other selections, we're tempted to say luck.

T A B L E   4–1

Security	Return
A	2%
B	2%
C	–1%
D	2%
E	2%
F	–1%
G	2%
H	–2%
I	3%
J	141%

Cases like this do occur. It's not unusual for the manager with the highest return for a given period to be one who happened to pick a security that significantly outshines the others. A single lucky bet is often only a short term success, rarely repeated. In this analysis, we can clearly see what the manager's above-average return is attributed to—one stock's outstanding return.

We may also want to look at the portfolio from an industry perspective to see if the manager's success (or failure) was due to any one or two industries that had significantly strong (or weak) performance.

SEGMENT CONTRIBUTIONS TO OVERALL PERFORMANCE

A manager may want to determine how each of the portfolio's segments contributed to the portfolio's overall return. This can be fairly straightforward, using the following formula:

$$W_{Pa} \cdot R_{Pa} = C_{Pa}$$

where

W_{Pa} = the weight (or percentage) invested in Sector A of the portfolio (at the beginning of the period)

R_{Pa} = the rate of return for Sector A of the portfolio

C_{Pa} = the contribution of Sector A to the portfolio's overall return

T A B L E   4–2

Segment Contributions to Portfolio Performance			
Industry Segment	**Rate of Return**	**Weight**	**Contribution**
Consumer Products	3.84%	8%	0.31%
Industrial Products	−11.52%	14%	−1.61%
Transportation	5.09%	12%	0.61%
Utilities	6.57%	7%	0.046%
Merchandising	8.30%	15%	1.25%
Financial Svcs	4.75%	9%	0.43%
Banks	−11.60%	11%	−1.28%
Conglomerates	3.50%	6%	0.21%
Technology	14.06%	10%	1.41%
Telecommunications	6.85%	8%	0.55%
Overall Portfolio	2.33%	100%	2.33%

The beginning period weight is used because that is when the manager presumably decides how to invest her client's money. The ending weight reflects the market change. Managers will typically adjust their weightings at various intervals (monthly, quarterly) either to rebalance the portfolios (i.e., bring them back into balance with their weighting strategy) or to adjust the balance (to reflect new thinking or new strategy). Please note that in this case the sum of the contributions equals the portfolio's rate of return.

This exercise helps identify how each segment contributed to the overall performance. This exercise can be done to diagnose any aspect of the portfolio.

STOCK OR INDUSTRY SELECTION

Managers typically invest in a particular style, relative to a benchmark. For example, the manager may be a *small cap* manager, meaning he invests in stocks with relatively low market capitalizations. There are hundreds of companies the manager may invest in. The decision as to what particular companies to buy is referred to as stock selection. This is one of the elements of performance attribution. That is, to determine what portion of the portfolio's return can be attributed to the manager's selection of stocks.

Another aspect of performance attribution is *industry selection,* also referred to as *timing.* This is essentially the *weighting* of the various industry types that comprise the portfolio, that is, the amount the manager has invested in the various industry types.

For example, 10% of a benchmark the manager is being measured against may be invested in technology stocks. Any deviation from this percentage is *industry selection* or *timing.* If the manager overweights technology (by investing more than 10% of the portfolio in technology), it's probably because she feels that technology stocks will do well. Underweighting (investing less than 10%) suggests the opposite.

Table 4–3 compares a portfolio's performance relative to its benchmark. I've labeled the columns to more easily explain how information is derived.

A review of the Portfolio Contribution column (Column E) reveals how each segment contributed (positively or negatively) to the portfolio's overall performance. Technology made the greatest positive contribution (1.41%), while Industrial Products had the greatest negative impact (1.61%). Contribution is the result of multiplying ROR times weighting.

Columns H and I show the effect of the manager's decisions on the results. These formulas are:

Industry Selection
$= Index\ ROR \cdot (Funding\ Weighting - Index\ Weighting)$

$Stock\ Selection = Portfolio\ Weighting \cdot (Portfolio\ ROR - Index\ ROR)$
$= Column\ C \cdot (Column\ A - Column\ B)$

$= Column\ B \cdot (Column\ C - Column\ D)$

The overall results show that stock selection had a positive effect on the success of the manager, while industry selection detracted from this success. The net difference equals the difference between the portfolio's and index's performances.

MORE DETAILED PERFORMANCE ATTRIBUTION ANALYTICS

Brinson, Hood, and Beebower discussed four components of portfolio performance in an article they wrote for the *Financial Analysts Journal.*[1] This methodology is rather straightforward and

TABLE 4–3

Sample Portfolio Performance Attribution[1]

Industry Segment	Rate of Return		Weight		Contribution			Management Effect	
	Portfolio	Index	Portfolio	Index	Portfolio	Index	Difference	Stock Selection	Industry Selection
	A	B	C	D	E	F	G	H	I
Consumer Products	3.84%	3.75%	8%	6%	0.31%	0.23%	0.08%	0.01%	0.08%
Industrial Products	−11.52%	−14.00%	14%	9%	−1.61%	−1.26%	−0.35%	0.35%	−0.70%
Transportation	5.09%	5.21%	12%	11%	0.61%	0.57%	0.04%	−0.01%	0.05%
Utilities	6.57%	6.20%	7%	10%	0.46%	0.62%	−0.16%	0.03%	−0.19%
Merchandising	8.30%	8.00%	15%	12%	1.25%	0.96%	0.29%	0.05%	0.24%
Financial Svcs	4.75%	4.50%	9%	8%	0.43%	0.36%	0.07%	0.02%	0.05%
Banks	−11.60%	−12.00%	11%	12%	−1.28%	−1.44%	0.16%	0.04%	0.12%
Conglomerates	3.50%	3.10%	6%	9%	0.21%	0.28%	−0.07%	0.02%	−0.09%
Technology	14.06%	10.11%	10%	13%	1.41%	1.31%	0.09%	0.40%	−0.30%
Telecommunications	6.85%	5.50%	8%	10%	0.55%	0.55%	−0.00%	0.11%	−0.11%
Overall Portfolio	2.33%	2.18%	100%	100%	2.33%	2.18%	0.14%	1.00%	−0.86%

[1]Please recognize that rounding will cause some results to be slightly different than might be expected.

provides an effective way to evaluate the impact of asset allocation and security selection decisions on a portfolio's performance.
These components are represented in Figure 4–1.

Quadrant I represents policy. This policy reflects the fund's
long-term asset allocation plan. The fund's benchmark return
would go here. Policy identifies the plan's normal portfolio. This
return is a result of the plan sponsor's investment policy.

Quadrant II reflects policy and timing's return effects. Timing
is the strategic decisions regarding the variations in asset class
weightings relative to the normal weight. Decisions that result in
adjustments to these weights are made to achieve a higher return
and/or lower risk.

Quadrant III represents policy and security selection returns.
Security selection deals with the active selection of investments
within an asset class.

Quadrant IV holds the actual return to the total fund for the
period. This is the result of the segment weights and returns.

The formulas for calculating these values are as follows:

$$Quadrant\ I: \sum_i (Wpi \cdot Rpi)$$
$$Quadrant\ II: \sum_i (Wai \cdot Rpi)$$
$$Quadrant\ III: \sum_i (Wpi \cdot Rai)$$
$$Quadrant\ IV: \sum_i (Wai \cdot Rai)$$

F I G U R E   4–1

		Selection	
		Actual	**Passive**
Timing	**Actual**	(IV) Actual Portfolio Return	(II) Policy and Timing Return
	Passive	(III) Policy and Security Selection Return	(I) Policy Return (Passive Portfolio Benchmark)

where:

Wpi = policy (passive) weight for asset class I
Wai = actual weight for asset class I
Rpi = passive return for asset class I
Rai = active return for asset class I

We can derive performance attribution results as follows:

Due to timing (asset allocation): Quadrant II – Quadrant I
Due to stock selection: III – I

Other	IV – III – II + I
Total	IV – I

Let's have an example:

A manager and plan sponsor have defined a portfolio's asset mix to be as follows:

Equities = 60%

Fixed Income = 40%

The actual makeup is

Equities = 55%

Fixed Income = 30%

Cash Equivalents = 15%

The equity benchmark for the portfolio is the Wilshire 5000, whose return for the period being evaluated was 28.3%. The portfolio's returns for this period are shown in Table 4–4.

Using the notation introduced earlier, we have the following for stocks:

$$Wp_{stocks} = 0.60$$
$$Wa_{stocks} = 0.55$$

T A B L E   4–4

Stocks	37.5%
Fixed-Income	20.0%
Cash Equivalents	7.1%
Total	26.6%

$$Rp_{stocks} = 0.283$$
$$Ra_{stocks} = 0.375$$

We can therefore calculate the four quadrants for the equity segment:

Quadrant I $= 0.60 \cdot 0.283 = 0.170 = 17.0\%$
Quadrant II $= 0.55 \cdot 0.283 = 0.156 = 15.6\%$
Quadrant III $= 0.60 \cdot 0.375 = 0.225 = 22.5\%$
Quadrant IV $= 0.55 \cdot 0.375 = 0.206 = 20.6\%$

The performance attribution piece then follows:

Due to timing $= 0.156 - 0.170 = -0.014 = -1.4\%$
Due to selection $= 0.225 - 0.170 = -0.055 = 5.5\%$
Other $= \underline{0.206 - 0.225 - 0.156 + 0.170} = -0.005 - 0.5\%$
Total $= 0.206 - 0.170 = 0.036 = 3.6\%$

Although the equity segment outperformed the benchmark by 9.2%, the segment's contribution to the overall portfolio return must be factored by its allocation (55%), thus resulting in a return of 20.6%. The segment's policy return (28.3% · 60%) is adjusted as well and yields a contributing return of 17.0%.

The attribution analysis shows that *timing* (that is, the asset allocation decision) affected the segment's return in a negative fashion. The manager decided to underweight this segment relative to policy, and as a result the portfolio's overall return suffered.

Stock selection contributed to the success of this segment. (Another negative effect [other] is undefined). These three values when added together equal the difference between the equity segment's contribution to the portfolio relative to the benchmark.

Performance attribution for fixed-income sectors could have additional factors, including maturity and duration, that would be taken into account and explained as part of the attribution process.

GLOBAL PORTFOLIOS

Additional factors are introduced with global investing. Here, the manager not only has to decide on individual stock selection, industry selection, and weightings, but also currency, market, and country allocations.

Once we invest a U.S.-based client's assets in another country, we introduce new variables. If we convert his U.S. dollars into yen, for example, and purchase a Japanese stock, our performance is not based simply on the return of the stock. Eventually, we'll sell the stock and convert the yen back into dollars. If, during the intervening period, the stock went up 10% but the yen depreciated versus the dollar, our conversion will yield less dollars than had the currency rates stayed the same. Alternatively, had we purchased stock that didn't do well but the currency situation favored us, we could yield a superior return based on the currency factor.

Often, managers recognize that they have a difficult enough time picking stocks without worrying about the currency market. Consequently, they may elect to currency hedge[2] their position to avoid problems with currencies. Such an action can neutralize the effect of currency on our portfolio, so we're only concerned with the individual stock's performance.

In an unhedged position, the influence of currency on our portfolio's return can be significant. Our manager may have picked a good security, but the conversion back to dollars may have caused us to suffer. Or the manger may not have been a good *stock picker*, but the currency rate change may have been in our favor.

Some firms employ multiple managers—some to concentrate on the currency situation and others to focus on stocks. The currency manager may elect to keep cash in multiple currencies, to take advantage of the short-term interest rate opportunities in the various countries. When it comes to hedging, the manager may elect a cross-hedging situation (e.g., for the purchase of a yen-based security, the dollars may be hedged against British sterling, which was used to convert to yen). Clearly, this additional dimension can add new opportunities (and complexities) to a portfolio's return.

Attribution helps clients and consultants separate market effect from skill. A manager's claim to be a good *stock picker* can be validated by doing the right kind of attribution analysis.

As one might expect, the derivation of global performance attribution is significantly more complicated than what I've presented above. For those readers who wish to explore this topic in greater detail,[3] the bibliography in the Selected References section at the end of this book contains sources that provide such details.

CHAPTER SUMMARY

Managers, investment consultants, and clients want to know where a manager's performance results came from. Did the manager pick the right stocks or was his success (or failure) due to poor weightings? Attribution analysis is one way of helping solve this riddle.

With the information we've provided, you should be able to determine how much of a manager's success is due to stock selection and how much to timing, or industry/asset selection.

ENDNOTES

1. Brinson et al. [1995], pp. 133–148.
2. Please refer to "Hedging" in the glossary for a brief explanation.
3. See Karnosky and Singer [1994] and Singer [1996].

CHAPTER 5

Style Analysis

One area of performance analysis that has come into vogue is the evaluation of the investment style, philosophy, or way of investing that a manager employs. A manager may claim to be investing in a particular style, but further investigation may reveal an inconsistency. We'll discuss some of the concepts behind this topic and one of the methods for analyzing style.

BACKGROUND AND PURPOSE

This attention to style analysis began in the 1970s, as the industry realized that there were varying philosophies or approaches to investing, which resulted in some level of uniformity in approach and results. Different investment styles will result in varying portfolio characteristics and, as a result, different performance patterns.

The performance of managers with similar styles should, on average, be more alike than the broader market or those managers who follow different investment styles. This is reasonable since these managers share similar portfolio characteristics and risks.

Style classification serves several purposes:[1]

1. Style is an important part of the design and maintenance of a diverse investment strategy, something that's rather typical with large pension plans.

2. It's a helpful tool when conducting searches for investment managers to fill the various roles in the plan's strategy.

3. It's an effective tool to validate that a manager is adhering to her stated style and the role she is playing in the overall strategy.

4. They provide a more effective way to evaluate performance.

Many clients establish performance-based fee arrangements with their manager. These arrangements tie performance to a benchmark. Superior performance results in a bonus, while under-performance will result in the base fee being paid or possibly a penalty being assessed. It's important to ensure that the investment style remains consistent with the agreed-upon benchmark, otherwise the manager may take on additional risk to achieve higher levels of performance.

Manager performance has often been compared with the broad market (e.g., S&P 500). While one might argue that a manager should "beat" the broad market more often than not, his style may be one that is cyclical and he may be underperforming the broader market for some period. Therefore, should the manager be compared with the broad market or the benchmark that more closely maps to his style? The investment community seems to favor the latter as the appropriate way of evaluating the manager's investment skills.

A passive fund manager provides an investment style that should correlate almost perfectly with an agreed-upon benchmark. The active manager brings two things to the table: investment style and investment skill. Since the investment skill is constrained within the bounds of the manager's style, doesn't it make sense to get a good understanding of the style the manager is employing?

Systematic or market risk is the risk of the market or, more specifically, the particular style. Issue risk is the risk attributable to each issue. It is also referred to as nonsystematic risk. If the return from style is calculated properly, then the following is true: Portfolio Total Return—Return from Style = Return from Issue Selection.[2]

Plan sponsors often split their funds across multiple managers, using a diversified approach based on investment styles. When searching for a manager, they will define the *style* they are interested in. The sponsor or their investment consultants will then conduct a search using the style as a way to segment the market.

Such terms as *fundamental, quantitative, growth, value, top-down, bottom-up,* and *sector rotator* are often used to reflect an aspect of a manager's style. Ann Posey, in her article in *Pension Management,*[3] defined a manager's style as "a set of prominent investment characteristics that the manager's portfolios persistently exhibit." These characteristics are "measurable financial attributes of the portfolio that are correlated significantly with its returns."

For equity managers, a portfolio's average market capitalization (cap), dividend yields, or earnings growth prospects may be employed. In the case of fixed-income managers, such values as the portfolio's duration or quality rankings may be used.

Frank Russell Company defines four broad categories for stocks:

- Value
- Growth
- Market-oriented
- Small-capitalization

The value style manager focuses on price, looking for opportunities when stocks are "cheap." There are four subcategories to this style:

- Low P/E
- Contrarian
- Yield

"P/E" represents the price-earnings ratio. This is a statistic that is often used in investing. The Low P/E manager is attracted to companies with low prices relative to earnings.

The contrarian managers are a bit more aggressive. They consider companies that have depressed earnings, where a turn-around is possible. While the quality of these companies is typically below average, the opportunities for reward can be great if the bet pays off.

Yield managers focus on the earnings of their investments. As a result, they tend to be more conservative than the other value managers.

Growth managers are looking for companies that offer above-average opportunities for growth. There are two substyles of growth managers:

- Consistent growth
- Earnings momentum

Growth managers are not necessarily interested in income. They may be buying a stock with little or no dividends, anticipating profits that will be derived through capital gains (by selling a stock and getting a profit).

Equity managers are often compared along two metrics: value-to-growth and capitalization. Various software packages exist that can help analyze a manager's style against these metrics and will plot the results in a grid similar to Figure 5–1.

MUTUAL FUND STYLE ANALYSIS

Mutual funds are often defined along various styles. This helps individuals decide which funds to invest in. The challenge is that in many cases the *style* a fund has claimed is, in reality, not consistent with what others consider that style to be. Consequently, an individual may *think* she's investing in one style when, in fact, she's investing in something very different.

Some of the equity styles that may be familiar to the reader include small cap, mid cap, large cap, growth, aggressive growth, income, and capital appreciation. Organizations such as Lipper Analytical have defined what they believe these terms mean and compare mutual funds against them. They then categorize the funds by their definitions, which can result in a fund being slotted

F I G U R E   5–1

	Value to Growth	
Large to Small	Large Value	Large Growth
	Small Value	Small Growth

differently than the portfolio manager may have intended. Nevertheless, this grouping can help investors do a better job of comparing one fund with another.

Assuming we have grouped funds or managers correctly by style, we can then compare them against each other, thus assessing each manager's investment skill. Identifying the appropriate style also allows us to pick a benchmark that is representative of that style, again affording us the opportunity of evaluating the manager's skill. Posey defines a benchmark as "a passive, investable representation of the manager's prominent investment characteristics. Fundamentally, it represents the manager's area of expertise—the group of securities, appropriately weighted, from which the manager typically selects a portfolio. In a broader sense, a benchmark reflects all investors with similar business interests, knowledge bases, risk tolerances and operating constraints."[4]

The difference between the benchmark's and manager's returns (excess return) reflects the skill the manager is offering. Since investors can often buy a benchmark through an index or passive manager, the active manager is chosen in hopes that her skill will result in superior results relative to the benchmark.

Style analysis is important because the investor wants to make sure she's placing her money with a manager whose investment approach is consistent with that of the generally accepted characteristics of the style he lays claim to. Various software firms offer products that can be used to confirm a portfolio's style by analyzing its characteristics. These systems provide greater accuracy in confirming style and detecting style shifts.[5]

Another aspect of style analysis is to compare the risk of the benchmark with that of the portfolio, to determine if the manager is taking more or less risk. There are various approaches to this.[6]

RETURN-BASED STYLE ANALYSIS

The theory behind return-based style analysis was developed by William F. Sharpe, a Nobel Prize winner in economic science. His theory states that a manager's past and present style can be determined by comparing her returns with a number of indexes. This approach is felt to be simplistic, fast, and accurate.

Here, we use the value R-squared, or R^2. This book is not intended to be a statistics text. However, to put it simply, this value is derived by subtracting the ratio of *unexplained variance* over the *total variance* from one, or

$$r^2 = 1 - \frac{unexplained\ variance}{total\ variance}$$

Consequently, a high number would suggest minimal unexplained variance. If we compare A with B, and have a high R-squared, we would conclude that these two values are closely correlated.

The return pattern of the manager is compared separately with each index. The squared correlation (R^2) between the manager's returns and the index is calculated. For example, let's say we did such a comparison against five indexes (see Table 5–1). Since the S&P 500 has the highest R-squared value (84.3%), we conclude that the manager is a U.S. domestic equity manager.[7]

Next, we want to determine the manager's specific style. As we did before, we'll limit this to small value, small growth, large value, and large growth. We would again calculate the R^2, this time against style indexes for these styles. We get the results shown in Table 5–2. From these results, we would conclude that ours is a large growth, U.S. domestic manager (because this style has the highest R-squared).

In an actual return-based style analysis, we would use many more indexes. Given the amount of data involved, we would want to use a software package to speed the process and ensure accuracy.

Some question the efficacy of this approach. One argument follows that managers who employ a particular style will select unique samples of securities from the style index. Given the variability of returns within the style, it's likely that each manager will

T A B L E   5–1

Index	r^2
Corporate Bond Index	4.2%
High-Yield Bond Index	17.3%
EAFE	21.3%
Russell 3000	67.3%
S&P 500	84.3%

TABLE   5–2

Style Index	r^2
Small Value	76.3%
Small Growth	81.2%
Large Value	87.3%
Large Growth	92.4%

achieve varying returns. Over time, one would expect the managers' average returns to correlate to their index return. However, this may not be true in all cases or for the short term. Christopherson and Trittin state that "correlation analysis can induce factor identification error and, by extension, plan risk. This error occurs because the correlation analysis cannot tell the difference between noise and true factor exposures."[8]

CHAPTER SUMMARY

Style analysis will continue to grow in importance. It benefits the manager, consultant, and plan sponsor. We've introduced the basic concepts and rationale behind this topic.

Investors want to make sure their manager is performing in the style that was agreed to, otherwise clients may be exposed to greater risks than they planned for. Also, comparison to a benchmark makes sense only if the benchmark correlates with the style of the investing.

Techniques such as risk-based style analysis afford many benefits. Sophisticated software packages now permit quick reviews of prospective managers, helping consultants and plan sponsors make their manager allocation decisions.

ENDNOTES

1. Christopherson and Tritten [1995].
2. Ryan Labs [1996].
3. Posey [1996] pp. 32–35.
4. Ibid., p. 33.
5. In the January 6, 1997, issue of *Pensions & Investments,* Steve Hardy wrote an article that challenged the excess return of a particular index fund relative to its benchmark ("Excess return for index fund ...," p. 10). The fund achieved a 160-basis-point

overperformance. Since an index fund is supposed to track an index or benchmark, there should be no excess performance. As Mr. Hardy points out, if anything there should be a slight underperformance to account for transaction costs (commissions) and advisory fees. By using his style analysis software, he determined that the fund didn't match the characteristics of the index it was being compared with. Instead, he uncovered other indexes it correlated much more closely with. When compared with these indexes, the returns were much more in line with the indexes.

6. Sortino [1996], pp. 22–26.

7. Perhaps there is some other index that would provide a higher R^2, but for our example, we're limiting the analysis to these five.

8. Christopherson and Trittin [1995], p. 76.

CHAPTER 6

Risk and Performance Measurement

"All of life is the management of risk, not its elimination."
—Walter Wriston, former chairman of Citicorp

In spite of the fact that risk measurement has been discussed for years, only fairly recently has it received the attention it deserves. This is probably due in part to the '87 stock market *adjustment*, the financial crisis at Barings, and other similar events. Investors have begun to realize that significant increases in returns may result from taking increased risks, but with the potential for significant losses. This chapter will discuss risk from a variety of viewpoints.

THERE'S NO SHORTAGE OF RISK

It seems that as we progress, we identify many new areas of risk. Here are just a few that investors are concerned with:

Interest Rate Risk

Purchasing Power Risk

Business Risk

Financial Risk

Liquidity Risk

Market Risk

Issue Risk

Default Risk

Credit Risk

Currency Risk

Country Risk

Political Risk

Economic Risk

Balancing the trade-offs between risk and return is a critical aspect of the investment process. To evaluate an investment manager's results fairly, it's important not only to look at the rate of return but also at the risk that was taken to achieve that return. As Paul Kaplan accurately states, "There is a fundamental difference between risk and return: return is what *did* happen, risk is what *could* have happened" (*emphasis added*).[1]

What is risk? The chance of losing something, be it our health, home, life, loved ones, or money. Our focus is, of course, on the risk of losing one's wealth. Risk combines uncertainty with the probability of loss. Uncertainty with no loss (e.g., finding a lottery ticket) involves no risk, nor do situations where loss is certain.

Let's expand on this a moment. What's the difference between an individual who *buys* a lottery ticket and one who *finds* a lottery ticket? The first has put some money at risk, while the other has made no such commitment. They both (in theory) have the exact same odds of winning, but the first stands to lose her investment, while the second will lose nothing should his ticket not have the right combination of numbers.

The second point is that if you *know* some loss will occur, you are at no risk.

Let's imagine for a moment the following scenario:

You've discovered a new investor who appears to have a superior track record for generating returns, so you give her $100,000 to invest. The first month you're told your investment has grown by 20% "Wow, 20%!" you respond.

For several months, your returns range from 15% to 20%. Then one month you're told that your entire investment has been wiped out! "How could this happen?" you ask.

"Well, I had a hard eleven showing against the dealer's four, so I doubled down. I was dealt a three. His hole card was a seven; he got a King and that was it. I was wiped out."

"Wait a minute, you were betting my investment at the black-jack table?"

Okay, a bit far-fetched, perhaps. But it illustrates the fact that there's always some element of risk involved in investing.

THE EMOTIONAL SIDE OF RISK

The intent of this chapter is to provide information on measuring risk. However, before doing so it's worth spending time discussing its emotional side.

It should be obvious that everyone has their own view of risk. For example, there are those who enjoy skydiving, while others ask "why would anyone jump out of a perfectly good airplane?" "The psychological literature indicates that investors not only behave irrationally and inconsistently over time, but also often form their own idiosyncratic risk measures *while* they are reviewing the data. No single predetermined measure can handle this situation."[2]

While I was working on this book, my wife and I had a brief discussion on risk. I posed this scenario to her: You have a choice, you can take $25 or have a 50/50 chance of winning $50 or nothing. Mathematically, the expected value[3] for either option is the same: $25. However, there are some (like the author) who would be willing to take the second option, while others (like the author's wife) would prefer to have the $25 ("a bird in the hand is worth ...").

I decided to raise the potential gain for the second option. We determined that somewhere around $125, she'd be willing to take the second option (i.e., a guaranteed $25 or a 50/50 chance to win $125). There are probably individuals who would go the other way (e.g., be willing to forgo a guaranteed $25 for the chance to win $40).

An individual's comfort with risk can be altered by a variety of circumstances. Someone who would normally be willing to risk ending up with zero might be inclined to take the guaranteed $25 if he hadn't eaten a meal in a few days (i.e., had fallen on hard times).

A classic example of risk is the plank that's placed on a floor with a large sum of money at one end. Who would be willing to walk the plank from one end to the other to claim the money? Most people would, since the risk of falling would most likely not result in an injury. But if you place the plank across the space between the roofs of two 10-story buildings, the number of takers will diminish sharply.

Let's introduce one further factor and see what happens. Instead of a pile of money, your child is at the other end and that building is on fire. What parent *wouldn't* walk across the plank to save his or her child?

So what's the point? Risk measurements provide a number that can be used to assess the risk of an investment option. However, the emotional side can't be overlooked. It will be unique for each individual and can vary due to circumstances the money manager simply can't control. As Peter Bernstein wrote in *Against the Gods—The Remarkable Story of Risk*, "Gut rules the measurement. Ask passengers in an airplane during turbulent flying conditions whether each of them has an equal degree of anxiety. Most people know full well that flying … is far safer than driving in an automobile, but some passengers will keep flight attendants busy while others will snooze happily regardless of the weather."[4] Bernstein goes onto say, "Risk is no longer something to be faced; risk has become a set of opportunities open to choice."[5] Risk measurements provide the investor with information she can use to help her decide whether or not the choice is worth the risk.

Risk is a relative concept, not an absolute one. If a pension fund requires a certain income level to meet its obligations to beneficiaries, falling below that level is unacceptable. Certain risk measures don't adequately address this kind of concern and are therefore unacceptable.

KINDS OF RISK

Investing money in securities involves a variety of risks. First, there's the risk in the individual corporation. We can call this *firm risk.* Will the company survive or succeed? Will it achieve our growth expectations? Are the right people running the company? Fundamental managers typically assess this level of risk by reviewing a firm's financial reports, visiting with the firm's officers, and conducting other types of reviews. A host of financial tools and measures are available to the analyst or portfolio manager to study a company's fundamentals.

Second, there's *industry risk.* This is a broader extension of firm risk. Since there's often a correlation between an individual firm's success and the success of the industry, it's wise to address the industry, too. What are the dynamics of the industry? Is it cyclical? What are its overall growth expectations? Are new companies entering the industry (e.g., computer software) or is it fairly stable (e.g., automotive)?

Third, there's economic risk. What's going on with the economy? How do changes in the economy affect the company or industry (e.g., does this company or industry do well in a recession?)?

International investing has introduced additional risks. For example, there's *country risk*. What's the stability of the country? Is it subject to civil strife? Does it honor its debt obligations? Is the government friendly to corporations and outside investing?

Of course, our focus is the risk to the security and the portfolio. However, I thought it would be helpful to outline that there are *numerous* risks that the company faces.

TWO ELEMENTS OF RISK

Mathematical models are used to come up with a numerical representation of risk. The possible outcomes may be plotted to assess the range of opportunities, both positive and negative.

There are two elements of risk that should be addressed. First, what is the risk of the investment? If you're betting on the *roll of the dice*, or some similar gambling scenario, you stand to lose quite a bit. You can also make quite a bit.

As we know, the odds at the gambling establishments in Las Vegas or Atlantic City are not with the gambler, otherwise these places would be out of business. They *must* have an advantage.

There are some situations where you can either lose your entire investment or receive some return (perhaps a doubling of your money). In situations like this, you need to determine the probability of success in order to determine whether or not the investment is a reasonable one.

The various state lotteries are set up to favor the state (again, this is because the state is looking to make money from these ventures). If you pick a three-digit number in a *pick three* or similar lottery game, your odds of winning are 1 in 1,000.[6] But is your return 1,000 to one (i.e., will you get 1,000 times your investment)? The answer is, of course, no. In most states, your return is 500 times the investment.[7]

Consequently, the odds are very much against a long-term participant in such a lottery making more money than he invests. In fact, over time the expected return is negative.[8]

At the other extreme are more "secure" investment approaches. You can, for example, invest your money in a savings account at your federally guaranteed bank. Or you might purchase Treasury bills. Because of the U.S. government's "guarantee" behind these investments, we refer to them as *riskless* or *risk-free* investments.

But in reality, are they without risk? What if the U.S. government *goes bust* or we're attacked by another country? The United States *has* defaulted on certain interest payment obligations, so there's always some element of risk, albeit a very, very slight one.

We've briefly discussed two very extreme examples of risk. The second important element that comes into play when discussing risk is the return relative to the risk, that is, the amount you're expected to realize based on the risk you're taking.

We know, for example, that in the case of the lottery, your return is 500 to 1, while your risk is one out of a thousand. As an investor, you must decide if this return justifies the risk you're taking. Can you handle such a risk? Is it warranted?

With a *secure* investment such as placing your money in a bank, your return can be quite small—2% or 3%, for example. Since you're not taking any risk, you can't expect much of a return. We'll now discuss some standard measurements that can be used to determine the risk of an investment.

MEASURES OF DISPERSION

Investment managers typically provide prospective clients with their average returns. These averages are a simple average or mean of the group of clients they manage money for. When hearing this number, many prospects assume this would be their expected return, while in reality had they had their investment with this manager for the period being discussed, the odds are probably as great that they would have had a higher return as that they would have had a lower return.[9]

So given that half the clients are above and half below the average, we will want to know how *close* to the reported average return our investment might have been. To determine this, we want to know the *dispersion* of returns about the average. Measures of dispersion indicate the scatter of the data—that is, how scattered or variable the data is around the reported average. The average values of two sets of data may be very similar, while the range and pattern of scatter differ greatly.

One very simple measure of dispersion is the *range* in client returns. By knowing the extreme points, you can assess how close your return may have been relative to the reported average.

A manager who reports an average return of 10% but whose worst performing client had a return of −20% and whose best was +30% would be thought to have quite a range of returns. Knowing this, you would have to decide if you could have lived with a −20% return. On the surface, it would appear that the manager isn't investing in a similar manner for each client, so how comfortable would you be with such a manager? A range from 8% to 12% is much closer than the earlier example, but may still be too broad for your liking.

STANDARD DEVIATION

One of the most common measures of risk is standard deviation, probably because it's relatively easy to calculate. Its use, however, is somewhat controversial. It's based on the normal distribution, which isn't normally applicable to a firm's clients.

Dr. Leslie Balzer was clear about his dissatisfaction when he wrote, "The greatest disservice done to standard deviation ... has been to call it *the* measure of investment risk ... it is a measure of uncertainty and that, as such, is *a* candidate for a risk measure. But uncertainty is not necessarily risk. It is uncertain whether I might win $1 million in a lottery, but that is hardly risk, unless one is concerned about how my attitudes and behavior might change if I did."[10]

Nevertheless, standard deviation is a widely used and accepted measure of dispersion and risk. AIMR has continued to include it as an accepted measurement.

We're all familiar with the *bell-shaped curve*. This curve shows the normal distribution of returns about the average. The farther out from the mean, the fewer the occurrences of a given return, and the lower the likelihood of achieving these returns. The range by itself doesn't convey enough information. We want to know how *tight* or *close* the returns are around the average. Standard deviation is an effective way to measure the degree of dispersion.

This statistical formula is quite common and relatively easy to determine. This measurement is also referred to as a measure of *volatility*, that is, we want to know how *volatile* or *variable* the returns are.

Here's a simple example. Two managers report identical average returns of 10% for a given period. From a risk standpoint, are they the same? Let's look at their client returns (see Table 6–1).

Each manager has ten clients. But, as you can see, their returns are quite diverse. Manager A's client returns range from –10% to +30%, while Manager B's range from 9% to 11%. While they both have average returns of 10%, and the likelihood of a client's return being above or below is the same, the variation in returns is quite large.[11]

The formula for calculating standard deviation is:

$$S_c = \sqrt{\frac{\Sigma[R_i - MEAN(R)]^2}{n}}$$

where

R_i = the return of the *i*th portfolio
$MEAN(R)$ = the arithmetic or simple average of all portfolios
n = the number of portfolios

TABLE   6–1

Manager A	Manager B
–10%	9%
–6%	9.2%
–2%	9.4%
+2%	9.6%
+6%	9.8%
+14%	10.2%
+18%	10.4%
+22%	10.6%
+26%	10.8%
+30%	11%

In Tables 6–2 and 6–3, we'll show how standard deviation is calculated for the two managers' clients shown above. First, manager A:

T A B L E   6–2

Returns (R_i)	$R_i - Mean(R)$	$[R_i - Mean(R)]^2$
−10	−10 − (10) = −20	400
−6	−16	256
−2	−12	144
+2	8	64
+6	4	16
+14	4	16
+18	8	64
+22	12	144
+26	16	256
+30	20	400
Sum of the squares =		1760

We now divide the *sum of the squares* by the average (10) and get 176. Finally, the standard deviation for this group of accounts is the square root of 176, or 13.27.

Approximately 68% of all items in a normal distribution are included between one standard deviation above and one standard deviation below the mean. For this manager, 68% of the returns are within the range from −3.27% to +23.27%.[12]

Now, for manager B:

T A B L E   6–3

Returns (R_i)	$R_i - Mean(R)$	$[R_i - Mean(R)]^2$
9	9 − (10) = −1	1
9.2	−0.8	0.64
9.4	−0.6	0.36
9.6	−0.4	0.16
9.8	−0.2	0.4
10.2	+0.2	0.4
10.4	+0.4	0.16
10.6	+0.6	0.36
10.8	+0.8	0.64
11	+1	1
Sum of the squares =		4.4

Dividing the *sum of the squares* yields 0.44. The standard deviation is the square root of this number, or 0.66. For Manager B, 68% of the clients had returns from 10 plus or minus 0.44, or from 9.56 to 10.44, a much *tighter* band than Manager A's.

A final comparison of these two managers is shown in Table 6–4. Since Manager A's standard deviation is higher than B's, Manager A is considered more risky.

The Sharpe Ratio

Another common measure of risk is the Sharpe ratio, which measures the excess return that a portfolio provides over the cash return, divided by the standard deviation of the portfolio's return. Another way of describing it is the excess return on a portfolio divided by the volatility of the securities. Its formula is:

$$S = \frac{r_b - r_f}{\sigma_p}$$

where

r_b = the portfolio return
r_f = the risk-free or cash return
σ_p = the standard deviation of the portfolio returns

Continuing with the earlier example, let's assume that the risk-free return is 5%. Measuring the Sharpe ratio for Manager A is simple:

$$S_A = \frac{.10 - .05}{13.27} = .0038$$

T A B L E   6–4

	Manager A	Manager B
Average Return	10%	10%
Range	−10% to +30%	9% to 11%
Standard Deviation	13.27	0.44
Range for 68% of clients	−3.27 to 23.27	9.56 to 10.44

And for Manager B:

$$S_A = \frac{.10 - .05}{.44} = .1136$$

Semivariance

One of the shortcomings of standard deviation is that it penalizes overperformance relative to the mean in the same way underperformance is penalized. Standard deviation doesn't differentiate between upside and downside volatility. As a result, funds that consistently produce high returns can have the same standard deviation as ones that produce low returns. This is illogical to many investors, who are really only concerned with poor performance, or what can be called *downside risk*.

An alternative is semivariance, which concerns itself only with those returns that fall below the mean or a target. Target semivariance focuses on returns that fall below a benchmark (perhaps the minimally acceptable rate of return for a plan).

By squaring the relative downside deviations, target semivariance penalizes the larger losses more than smaller ones. This is important, since many investors have greater concern with devastating losses than with smaller losses.

Target variance averages the squares of deviations from the target and only addresses itself with deviations below the target. Because target semivariance only addresses itself with undesirable outcomes, proponents claim it's a better risk measure than standard deviation. While this may have some appeal, some caution is due against this being the only measure. A string of high returns might indicate the eventual appearance of low returns.

Paul Kaplan and Marius Daugirdas cite the example of the Japanese stock market, which had positive but variable annual returns in every year from 1980 to 1989. It had a large negative return in 1990, which would not have been predicted with target semivariance. In this case, standard deviation would have been a more appropriate measure.[13]

Target semivariance[14] is a variation on this measurement. It measures dispersion of returns less than a specified target return, relative to the target. Consequently, it's a measure of *downside* risk.

The formula is as follows:

$$SV(t) = \Sigma_{Ri\sigma t}\, p_i\, (t - R_i)^2$$

where

R_i = a possible return
p_i = the probability of the actual return being R_i
t = the target return

A measure of semivariance should be based on a complete probabilistic model of portfolio returns. A time series should be used to estimate the model, and then the model should be used to estimate target semivariance.

Regression to the Mean

Peter Bernstein attributes the discovery of the concept of *regression to the mean* to Francis Galton, who defined essentially this principle as the tendency of *outliers* to move toward the mean.[15] Applying this to the world of investing, Bernstein suggests that today's success story will be tomorrow's failure, and vice versa: "When investors overreact to new information and ignore long-term trends, regression to the mean turns the average winner into a loser and the average loser into a winner."[16] He goes onto say, "The track records of professional investment managers are also subject to regression to the mean. There is a strong probability that the hot manager of today will be the cold manager of tomorrow, or at least the day after tomorrow, and vice versa."[17,18]

Value at Risk

A growing measure of financial risk is VAR, or value at risk. VAR summarizes the worst expected loss over a target horizon within a given confidence interval.

In a single number, VAR summarizes the global exposure to market risks and the probability of adverse moves in financial variables. It measures risk in something individuals are very comfortable with—dollars.

VAR can be used for financial reporting, setting trading position limits, measuring risk-adjusted returns, and model evaluation. Institutional investors are embracing VAR as a dynamic method for controlling risk exposure, especially when many outside managers are involved. VAR combines existing positions with risk estimates over the target horizon.

It's recommended that VAR be reported with confidence intervals. For example, if the one-month VAR with a confidence level of 95% on a $100 million portfolio is $6 million, there is a 95% chance that the worst possibility is a $6 million loss in value. More details regarding VAR can be found in Jorion [1996].

RISK MANAGEMENT

While the investment industry is trying to agree on the proper way to measure risk, a second factor comes into play—the management of risk. As *Global Investment Technology* reported, "The [Group of Thirty Global Derivatives Study Group's] report, 'Derivatives: Principles and Practices,' released in 1993, put senior management at financial institutions on notice that they could be held personally responsible for failing to monitor investment risk at their firms … the need for better risk management is rising to the fore."[19] As Bernstein points out, "The demand for risk management has risen along with the growing number of risks."[20]

Risk management involves *knowing* the risks, determining the acceptable level(s) of risks, defining appropriate measures for risks, validating these measures, and taking steps to monitor portfolios to ensure they're within the defined boundaries.

Part of the interview process with any new client involves an assessment of the client's risk tolerance. As stated earlier, each client will be willing to handle different levels of risk. The manager must understand the client's unique comfort level and then ensure that the client's investments fall within these guidelines.

Managers have a fiduciary responsibility to properly monitor risk exposure. The best way to do this is through a quantifiable mechanism. We've outlined a variety of measures above, since managers may find that multiple measurements are needed to manage risk properly.

CHAPTER SUMMARY

Risk measurement is an area that's filled with alternative viewpoints. It seems that everyone has valid reasons for using or not using one particular measure or another. As Kaplan and Daugirdas suggest, "No single measure of risk is perfect for all situations, making it all the more important that members of the pension industry continue to be aware of the limitation of each approach."[21]

We've discussed a variety of risk measures. It is unlikely that the investment industry will agree to a single measure, nor is it reasonable to expect that one measure would suffice.

Both portfolio managers and investors must recognize that with each investment, some level of risk is being taken. An assessment of the returns relative to risk is important to ensure that the realized returns are in line with these risks.

ENDNOTES

1. Kaplan [1996], pp. 40–44.
2. Balzer [1995], pp. 5–16.
3. Expected value is a statistical term. It has to do with the value one would expect to obtain over a period of time or given certain probable outcomes. In the example of the situation I posed to my wife, I asked her if she'd prefer to have $25 or a 50/50 chance of winning $50. The option of being handed $25 yields an expected value of $25, since we would be guaranteed the $25 payout (the probability of certainty is 100%; we multiply 100% (or 1.00) times the potential payout ($25): 1.00 * $25 = $25—our expected value). The real question is what is the likelihood of her winning $50— what's the expected value of this second option? Well, the odds are 50/50. We know she will either win (and get $50) or lose (and get zero). But from a pure probability standpoint, we would take the probability (50/50 = .50) and multiply it times the potential gain ($50). This yields our "expected value" of $25 (.50 * $50 = $25). While we know that this isn't what she's going to get, in determining which option to take, it's best (again, from a probability perspective) to calculate the expected value of the options, and then choose the option with the highest expected value. In this case, the expected values are identical—$25. A reason why expected values aren't always effective is that they're purely mathematical—they don't take into consideration the person's attitude toward risk. In the above case, while my wife preferred the *certainty* of getting $25, I would prefer to gamble on getting the $50. A statistician's recommendation would be to go with either option, based on the expected value result. When we bring a person's attitude toward risk into play, we can find behavior that is contrary to the statistical recommendation or guideline. For example, millions of people spend millions of dollars buying lottery tickets. The expected value of each purchase is less than their investment (given that 100% of the money being bet is not being distributed). Nevertheless, people are willing to take a gamble because they hold out hope that their next ticket will be a winner.

4. Bernstein, Peter L., *Against the Gods—The Remarkable Story of Risk*, p. 105.

5. Ibid., p. 110.

6. There are 1,000 possible combinations of numbers, ranging from 000 to 999.

7. State lotteries often replaced illegal "numbers" games that used to attract a lot of gamblers. It's interesting to note that these illegal operations typically had better payouts than the state (granted, their overhead wasn't as extensive and you had to factor in your probability of actually getting your winnings).

8. One might advise a lottery participant who wins early in her betting days to *quit while she's ahead*, since she's bound to give back all of her winnings and plus some over time. The odds are simply with the state, not the gambler.

9. After all, this is what an average is. The author recalls a time when a registered representative for an investment adviser he was working with called to complain that half his clients had returns that were below average. However, if half a firm's clients *aren't* below average, there's something wrong with the calculation!

10. Balzer [1995], pp. 5–16.

11. It's interesting to note that in both of these cases, not a single client had a return that equaled the reported average of 10%. We would expect that this would be the typical situation.

12. One might think that such a range is extreme and unusual, but the reality is that it isn't. I know of a firm whose composite statistics for one period were:
Average return   = 27.24%
Highest return   = 110.47%
Lowest return   = 8.1%
Standard deviation = 19.58.
Using standard deviation as our risk measure, 68% of their clients fell within 7.66% and 46.82%, a rather wide range, wouldn't you agree?

13. Kaplan, Paul D., and Marius Daugirdas, "Traditional vs. New Forms of Risk Measure," *Pensions & Investments*, November 25, 1996, p. 12.

14. Riepe, Mark W., and Scott L. Lummer, *Pension Investment Handbook*, Ibbotson Associates, pp. 11–34.

15. Bernstein, p. 167.

16. Bernstein, p. 175.

17. Bernstein, p. 175.

18. The November 22, 1996, edition of *The Wall Street Journal* reported on Brad Lewis of Fidelity Investments. "For years, the 41-year-old portfolio manager seemed to have a magic stock-picking machine." From 1989 through 1994, Lewis outperformed the S&P 500. Mr. Lewis would apparently boast that his fund was an "index killer" that could "consistently beat the index through astute, automated, and ever improved stock selection." The article reported that his fund is "headed toward its second straight year of trailing the S&P."

19. GIT [1994], p. 1.

20. Bernstein, p. 213.

21. Kaplan and Daugirdas [1996].

CHAPTER 7

The SEC and Performance Measurement

In general, the investment industry is relatively *self regulating*. However, The U.S. Securities and Exchange Commission (SEC) has guidelines governing various aspects of the industry, with much of these guidelines devoted to performance measurement. As one might imagine, much of this effort has been in the reporting of past performance results.[1] The SEC and its staff have articulated guidelines for the advertising of performance through a series of "no-action" letters[2] and enforcement actions. This chapter will provide some background into some of the SEC regulations and no-action letters that relate to performance measurement.

THE ADVISERS ACT

The SEC set forth its policies regarding advertising, including the advertising of performance information, under the general antifraud provision of the Investment Advisers Act of 1940, commonly referred to as the Advisers Act.

Section 206 makes it unlawful, "to employ any device, scheme or artifice to deceive, or manipulate any client or prospective client" or to "engage in any transaction, practice, or course of business which operates as a fraud or deceit upon any client or prospective client." The SEC has authority to define acts, practices, and courses of business that it feels fall under the category of being fraudulent, deceptive, or manipulative. The SEC may also establish rules to prevent fraud.

THE ADVERTISING RULE

Rule 206(4)-1 of the Advisers Act established rules regarding advertising. One deals with the definition of "advertisement." The Act defines it to include any

1. "notice, circular, letter or other written communication addressed to more than one person"
2. "notice or other announcement in any publication or by radio or television, which offers investment advisory service with regard to securities."

Another prohibition disallows any advertisement that

- refers to any testimonials concerning the adviser
- refers to past specific recommendations that were or would have been profitable unless the adviser complies with certain conditions
- provides formulas, graphs, charts, etc., that can be used for making trading decisions without proper disclosures regarding their use
- claims that a service is "free" unless it truly is

The Rule prohibits advertisements that are untrue, false, deceptive, or misleading.

The SEC's positions regarding performance advertising have evolved. For example, until the late '70s the SEC's position was that the use of actual or model results was "false or misleading." This has changed in favor of a "facts-and-circumstances" test. Whether the use of performance results is false or misleading is based on whether "it implies, or a reader would infer from it, something about the adviser's competence or about future investment results that would not be true had the advertisement included all material facts."

CLOVER CAPITAL MANAGEMENT, INC.

One of the most important no-action letters deals with Clover Capital Management (see Appendix B). This letter defines the following as being misleading (regarding the use of model or actual performance results):

1. fails to disclose the effect of market or economic conditions on the results portrayed (for example, if the advertisement touts the adviser's 25% return without disclosing that the market went up by 40%)

2. includes results without the deduction of advisory fees, commissions, and other expenses

3. fails to disclose whether or not the results reflect the reinvestment of dividends

4. suggests the potential for profit without disclosing the risk of loss

5. compares results with an index without disclosing all material facts about the comparison (e.g., not disclosing that the volatility of the index is materially different from that of the portfolio)

6. fails to disclose any material conditions, objectives, or strategies used to obtain the results (e.g., that the model is based on a particular style of investing)

7. fails to prominently disclose the model's limitations, particularly the fact that the results aren't based on actual trading but are a model

8. when applicable, fails to disclose that the model's conditions, objectives, or strategies changed materially during the time portrayed by the advertisement and the effect of any such change on the results

9. when applicable, fails to disclose that any of the model's securities or strategies do not or only partially relate to the type of advisory services currently offered by the adviser (e.g., if the model includes securities the adviser no longer recommends)

10. if applicable, fails to disclose that the adviser's clients had results that were materially different from the model's.

11. if applicable, fails to prominently disclose that the results relate only to a select group of the adviser's clients, which was the basis on which the selection was made, and the effect of this practice on the results.

In the Clover no-action letter, the SEC required that performance results be shown on a net-of-fee basis, that is, after fees have been deducted.

Performance results have typically been shown net-of-commissions, but the deduction of fees has been controversial. AIMR's standards, for example, recommend that gross-of-fee results be shown, as long as it's not in violation of the SEC rules.[3]

The SEC has since relaxed the Clover letter by allowing performance results to be shown without deducting custodial fees, since the client typically selects and pays the custodian.

ADVERTISEMENT OF PAST PERFORMANCE

The SEC issued a no-action letter to Horizon Asset Management that permits the advertising of performance results that a key employee achieved at a former firm. The key issue behind this decision was that the portfolio manager was the controlling manager at both his former firm and Horizon.[4]

The SEC position extends what was permitted in previous letters. For example, the SEC replied to a request by Fiduciary Management Associates that, with appropriate disclosure, the adviser could use the performance of the accounts that came with him to his new firm if no one other than the portfolio manager played a major role in the performance of client accounts and the performance of accounts that fell under his management at the new firm was not significantly different from the performance results of the accounts that did not follow him.

PORTABILITY OF PERFORMANCE

Due to the growth and competitiveness of the investment industry, portfolio managers often leave one firm to join or start another. Since their ability to attract new business can be tied to their prior success, these managers often want to include information on their prior activities in their advertising materials. The issue of *portability* of performance, or the ability of an investment adviser to take credit for the performance of a predecessor firm, is one that the SEC has addressed, due to the potential for misrepresentation and abuse.

In *Fiduciary Management Associates, Inc.*, an investment adviser led by a portfolio manager who was previously an officer of another firm sought assurances that the SEC staff wouldn't object if the adviser included the results of accounts managed by the portfolio manager while at the former firm.[5]

The SEC's position was that the adviser could use the returns for those accounts that followed the manager to the new firm, provided no one other than the portfolio manager played a significant part in the accounts' performance and that the performance results of any new accounts the manager took on at the new firm were similar to these older accounts. Appropriate disclosures would be necessary to reflect the use of this prior information.[6]

The SEC has taken a similar position regarding the purchase of one firm by another. The SEC essentially states that the use of prior performance results can be done if the manager who was previously responsible for those performance numbers continues to manage the accounts at the new firm.[7]

ASSOCIATION FOR INVESTMENT MANAGEMENT & RESEARCH

The SEC issued a no-action letter on December 13, 1996 (see Appendix C) in response to a request from the Association for Investment Management & Research (AIMR). As an advocate for the investment management industry, AIMR sought to obtain relief in the reporting of investment performance by managers under certain circumstances. I would suggest that two of the items addressed will have a major benefit to the industry.

First, AIMR addressed the issue of the reporting of gross-of-fee returns. AIMR (and its predecessor group, the Financial Analysts Federation, which initiated the effort that eventually led to the publication of AIMR's Performance Presentation Standards [AIMR-PPS™]) recommends that managers report their performance gross-of-fees, that is, before advisory fees are removed. The reason is fairly basic. Since most advisers charge fees based on asset size and other criteria, their clients will be paying a variety of fee rates. The aggregation of accounts into a composite will yield a net-of-fee (i.e., after fees are removed) return at a rate that may not be relevant to the prospective client. Gross-of-fee returns can be used by prospective clients as the starting point. Knowing the fee they would be charged, they can adjust the gross-of-fee return to determine an ROR appropriate to them.

The SEC previously insisted on net-of-fee results and only permitted the use of gross-of-fee returns in one-on-one situations. AIMR suggested a scenario under which the advertising and use of gross-of-fee returns in other than one-on-one situations might be acceptable. This included the requirement that both net- and gross-of-fee returns be shown together, with neither being shown in a predominant manner. Other criteria are outlined in Appendix C. The SEC concurred with AIMR's condition and now permits the reporting of gross-of-fee returns.

The second major outcome from this letter concerns the incorporation of mutual funds in composites. Since mutual funds qualify as fee paying, discretionary accounts, it is natural that they be included in one or more of a firm's composites. The difficulty arises when a firm wishes to provide gross-of-fee returns for these composites.

The SEC had required that mutual fund performance always be shown net-of-fee. AIMR argued that since the composite is being used to attract private accounts, not mutual fund accounts, the firm should be able to *gross-up* the funds so that gross-of-fee returns could be reported. Once again, AIMR specified the conditions under which this would take place, including the requirement that no funds included in the composite would be identified. Again, the SEC concurred with AIMR's conditions and now permits mutual fund returns to be calculated gross-of-fee when they're included in composites.

This does *not* permit firms to report gross-of-fee performance in advertisements or presentations of mutual funds. It is only intended for the inclusion of mutual funds in composites.

CHAPTER SUMMARY

One of the SEC's ultimate responsibilities is to ensure that investment managers aren't reporting returns that could be misleading, deceptive, or fraudulent. The basis for many of their decisions to take enforcement action are the various laws enacted by the U.S. Congress.

Because the industry can be quite complicated and numerous diverse situations can arise, the SEC often has to consider situations on a case-by-case basis. By issuance no-action letters the commission can indicate that under certain specified situations it won't take action.

Certain landmark no-action letters have been issued that encompass performance measurement. We've discussed two in particular, Clover Capital Management and the AIMR. Copies of these letters are contained in the appendices for those who wish to review them in greater detail.

ENDNOTES

1. Much of the information contained in this chapter was derived from presentation materials provided by Steven W. Stone and Lawrence P. Stadulis of Morgan, Lewis & Bockius LLP at their presentation at the National Regulatory Services, Inc.'s "Compliance Basic Training for Investment Advisers" seminar held in New York, NY, October 3, 1996.
2. See the Glossary for an explanation of no-action letters.
3. The SEC had only permitted gross-of-fee in one-on-one situations (e.g., an Investment Adviser's sales person meeting with a prospect), as long as the adviser provides at the same time:
   - a statement that the returns do not reflect the deduction of advisory fees
   - that the client's return will be reduced by advisory fees and any other expenses they might incur
   - an indication that the advisory fees are described in Part II of the adviser's Form ADV
   - a representative example (i.e., table, chart, graph, narrative) that shows the effect that an advisory fee could have on the total value of a client's portfolio

   These one-on-one presentations can actually be held with more than one individual, as long as it's "private and confidential" and made in a setting that affords each prospect the chance to discuss fees. Prospective clients that qualify for such meetings include high-net-worth individuals, pension funds, universities, and other institutions that have sufficient assets to justify the costs of one-on-one presentations. The 1996 No-Action Letter to AIMR expands this rule to allow *gross-of-fee* reporting in advertising, under certain conditions (see Appendix C) and below.
4. "Investment Advisers May Advertise Past Performance," by Mark Henderson, *Securities Industry News*, October 28, 1996, p. 5.
5. Stone [1996], p. 10.
6. Stone [1996], p. 10.
7. Stone [1996], pp. 11–12.

CHAPTER 8

An Overview of the Standards

In an attempt to achieve some uniformity in the calculation and reporting of performance measurement results, a variety of standards have been issued since the late 1960s. These standards have been developed and have evolved in response to changes in the industry. In this chapter, we'll discuss the main performance measurement (BAI and ICAA) and reporting (AIMR and IMCA) standards.

BACKGROUND—THE NEED FOR STANDARDS

Prior to 1968, there were no formal industry standards regarding any aspect of performance measurement. Most money management firms calculated rates of return using the internal rate of return (IRR) formula, but there was little consistency from one firm to another. As noted earlier, a shortcoming of the IRR is that it provides a *dollar-weighted rate of return*, not a *time-weighted* return. One might be inclined to ask, "Why are performance measurement standards necessary."

In spite of the fact that the Securities and Exchange Commission (SEC) requires the use of a caveat or disclaimer, stating that *past results are not necessarily an indication of future performance*, most investors rely heavily on past performance to decide on a money manager. Let's use a simple analogy to emphasize this point. Baseball players are often compensated on their ability to hit. Their *batting average* is a measurement that team owners and managers use to decide what players they want to attract. What if there were no standard method for calculating a player's batting average? The standard formula for calculating a batting average is:

$$Batting\ Average = \frac{Number\ of\ Hits}{Times\ at\ bat - (Walks + Hit\ by\ pitches)}$$

In other words, a batter isn't penalized for the occasions they come to bat and reach base because of a walk or because they're hit by a pitched ball. They will be penalized if they get on base because they hit the ball and a fielder makes an error (because they would have been out had the fielder not made the error). Here's an example:

Times at Bat	Hits	Walks	On Base Due to Error
12	4	2	2

Here, we would calculate the person's batting average as:

$$Batting\ Average = \frac{4}{12 - 2} = \frac{4}{10} = .400$$

But what if one team didn't exclude walks, or if another counted *any time* a batter reached base as a hit, even if it was the result of a fielding error?

$$Batting\ Average_{w/walks} = \frac{4}{12} = .333$$

$$Batting\ Average_{w/o\ errors} = \frac{4}{12 - 4} = \frac{4}{8} = .500$$

As you can see, we get different results depending on the method used (ranging, in this case, from .333 to .500). Comparing one batter with another would be difficult, if not impossible. The same problem could arise in comparing one manager with another, since there was no standard way of calculating performance.

The reality is that there have been vast differences in the way managers calculate individual performance and how they present performance to prospective clients. Let's take treatment of cash flows. Some managers assume that all cash flows occur in the middle of the month. While there are some inaccuracies with this method, it has been generally accepted as a reasonable approximation approach, as long as flows didn't exceed 10% of the account's market value. Other managers day-weight the flows. That is, their calculation gives greater emphasis to flows that occur in the beginning of the period than those occurring at the end. This is considered an improvement on the midmonth method. Again, it's an acceptable method.

The author came across an undated report from a rather large investment manager that stated, "For consistency, cash flow is calculated as if it came in at the end of the month, after the performance is calculated."[1]

The problem with this approach is that inflows will be treated as if they occurred at the end of the month. In cases where the flow actually occurred at the beginning, any return that would be rightly attributed to the flow will be erroneously assigned to the beginning period's market value. An equally erroneous event will occur when outflows actually take place at the beginning of the month. What's interesting is that this report's methodology was approved by a "big six" accounting firm.[2]

CALCULATING RATES OF RETURN—THE BANK ADMINISTRATION INSTITUTE

In 1968, based on the work of Peter Dietz, the Bank Administration Institute (BAI) published its standards document for calculating rates of return—*Measuring the Investment Performance of Pension Funds*. This document provided the investment industry with calculation standards strongly recommending the use of *time-weighted rates of return*.

The major difference between *dollar-weighted* and *time-weighted* returns is how they treat *cash flows*. Dollar-weighted returns are affected by cash flows, as shown in the example on page 21, while time-weighted returns are not. The BAI felt that it was unfair to reward or penalize a portfolio manager based on actions taken by his or her client.

The BAI report referenced a study that uncovered "a variety of meanings given to the word "performance."[3] It goes on to say that "the Advisory Committee ... are aware of the variety of conceptions of *performance* which are in use, [and] unanimously and strongly advocates that performance be measured by computing the actual rates of return on the pension fund's assets. Without exception, these rates of return should be based upon a determination of the *market value* of the fund's assets at different points in time ... The use of market value rather than book value is of extreme importance."[4]

The report went on to point out the shortcomings of the IRR, showing how it measures the performance of the *fund* rather than the performance of the fund's *manager*.

> This distinction arises because some of the things that affect the performance of the fund often are not under the control of the fund manager. Therefore, if the only measurement were of the performance of the fund, the fund manager might be unfairly blamed for poor results or might be applauded without justification for good results. The things which most frequently affect a fund's performance and which are often not controlled by the fund manager are the timing and amounts of cash flows between the trustor and the fund and between the fund and the beneficiaries. Since it can importantly affect a fund's performance, the influence of the timing of cash flows on the fund's performance must be eliminated in order to measure the performance of the fund's manager ... For this reason, the Committee recommends the use of the time-weighted rate of return for the purpose of measuring the performance of the managers or trustees of pension funds.[5]

The significance of the BAI standards was that for the first time the pension fund industry had standards on how to calculate rates of return. As suggested above, the industry previously had a variety of measures, including some that weren't even based on the market values of the fund's holdings.

The BAI standards went beyond the measurement of return to address several other issues.

1. Estimating Risk. The Committee encouraged the use of a risk measurement to be included along with the rate of return. Although the group recommended the use of the mean absolute deviation to measure variability, it acknowledged

that this area was subject to change and encouraged additional research and analysis to provide better risk measures.

2. Classifying Pension Funds. The BAI committee acknowledged the problems with comparing *apples and oranges* in trying to compare one fund's performance with another. In addition to identifying risk variations between funds, they also encouraged differentiating funds by purpose, contractual arrangements, and technical characteristics of funds, including size, age, and rate of growth.

3. Classifying Pension Fund Assets. Interest was growing for the measurement of performance at levels below the fund, to include various categories of assets. Assessing the performance at the asset level could be beneficial in diagnosing the reason for a pension fund's performance.

4. Valuation of Pension Fund Assets. The standards provided procedures for valuing a fund's assets, calling for the use of market values.

This effort was extremely important for the industry for several reasons. First, it set forth a standard approach for measuring rates of return. Plan sponsors and individuals seeking someone to manage their assets would be much better off by having such a uniform measurement. Anyone complying with the *BAI standards* could be compared much more easily.

The suggestion that funds be compared based on some degree of similarity encouraged the classification of styles and other differentiating characteristics. The BAI acknowledged that a rate of return by itself didn't convey enough information. A risk measure is necessary to fully appreciate the return and the likelihood of achieving similar returns in the future, as well as for comparing one manager with another.

Although the term *performance attribution* wasn't in vogue at the time, the idea of measuring performance at the subportfolio level was, in fact, a way of trying to attribute a fund's performance to its components. And finally, the requirement that funds be priced based on market values was important for assessing a manager's true performance.

Managers began to adopt these standards and the phrase "we're in compliance with the BAI standards" became rather common, thus providing plan sponsors a way of contrasting one manager with another without wondering how each arrived at their reported returns.

THE INVESTMENT COUNSEL ASSOCIATION OF AMERICA (ICAA)

The ICAA is an industry organization founded in 1937 that is comprised of independent investment advisers.[6] One might believe that although many of their members saw the BAI standards as being quite valuable, there was a sense that the investment advisory community should have their own set of standards. In reality, these standards were developed because of the need for a simpler approach to deriving time-weighted rates of return.

The BAI standards recommended the *linked internal rate of return* to calculate a time-weighted return. This formula still involved an iterative process that was best suited for a firm that had a large computer. Most investment advisory firms in the early 1970s didn't have such a computer (or for that point, any computer). So a simpler method was sought. The ICAA provided such a measure.

In 1971, the ICAA published their *Standards of Measurement and Use for Performance Data*. While the BAI published a very detailed and in-depth report, the ICAA provided a much more concise booklet with guidelines that were actually quite similar to those of the BAI.

1. Total Return. The ICAA required the inclusion of income when measuring a fund's return. It also recommended accruing income rather than incorporating income only when it is realized.

2. Rate of Return. Like the BAI, the ICAA pointed out the differences between the *dollar-weighted* and *time-weighted* rates of return, and required a time-weighted return based on the following formula:

$$R = \frac{V^2 - V^1 - C + I}{V^1 + 1/2C} * 100$$

where

V^1 = the beginning period market value
V^2 = the ending period market value
C = the net cash flow (from any source, including reinvested income)
I = the income for the measurement period
R = the rate of return

Unlike the *linked internal rate of return*, this formula involves no iterative process to derive the rate of return. Its simplicity was quite appealing to investment firms seeking to calculate a time-weighted rate of return on a monthly or quarterly basis.

3. Performance for Total Portfolio and Portfolio Segments. Like the BAI, the ICAA saw the benefit in providing segment-level rates of return.

4. Definitions within Portfolio Segments. Again, like the BAI, the ICAA discouraged comparisons of funds that were different in composition or other characteristics.

5. Total Time Period Shown. The ICAA suggested that managers report performance for a 5-year time period, with the minimum objective being the length of time for one market cycle (rising and falling markets).

6. Time Intervals Used. The ICAA touched on the reporting of performance, suggesting that for this 5-year time period, annual (1-year) returns be shown, as well as period (2-year, 3-year, etc.) be reported as well. At the time the FAF first proposed their performance presentation standards, the ICAA published their own presentations standards. Their's were similar to the FAF's, but with a number of differences (for example, the FAF required asset weighting of account performance while the ICAA encouraged equal weighting).

7. Variability of Returns. Although the ICAA standards didn't refer to this as a *risk measure*, like the BAI the ICAA called for a measure of dispersion. For the ICAA, it's standard deviation.

As a result of these two efforts, the money management industry now had two very similar sets of standards that primarily dealt with the *calculation* of rates of return.

PRESENTING PERFORMANCE RESULTS—ASSOCIATION FOR INVESTMENT MANAGEMENT & RESEARCH

Historically, managers have had a variety of ways to report performance to prospects. Here are just a few:

1. Model Account. A manager has a single account (real or fabricated) that is used to represent her investment skills. Whether the firm is managing 20, 200, or 2,000 accounts, a single account is used for publishing her past performance. The problem with a model should be fairly obvious. First, if the *model* is fabricated, there may not be any transaction costs[7] associated with the investments. There won't be any official records (trade tickets, brokerage or custodial statements) that can be used to validate the reported performance. If it's a single account, one might wonder what special treatment or care has gone in to ensure the account has superior performance.

   A question that should come to mind is *How truly representative of the rest of the accounts is the model account?* In most cases we suspect that this account's performance will be much higher than the average of the other accounts.

2. A Select, Stable Group of Accounts. Some managers create a group of accounts from which their performance is reported. While this might seem better than the *single-account* approach, this method has similar problems.

   One additional problem is the makeup of these accounts. Are they of a similar investment style or are they a mix? The author is aware of cases where the mix was truly a mix, with accounts coming from four to six very different investment styles. How representative could this group's average return be?

3. A Variable Group of Accounts. Some managers used to select their top five accounts for each measurement period. In other words, it was likely that this group would change each quarter. And clearly, this group's performance was anything but representative of the manager's overall success.

There have also been many other differences in the way managers reported performance to prospective clients. For example:

1. **Net or Gross of Fees.** Some managers reported performance after (net) management fees had been removed, while others reported the return before (gross) fees.

2. **Accruing for Income.** Some managers accrued for income while others realized it on a cash basis (only when the income had hit the account).

3. **Return's Relation to Prospect's Objectives.** Many (if not most) managers used a single return figure to represent their performance, although they may have managed in different ways based on the objectives, risk tolerance levels, and other characteristics of their clients. Others attempted to provide their clients with a return that came from accounts with backgrounds similar to theirs.

With these vast differences, how could a plan sponsor decide on a manager? The sponsor might have returns from ten different managers, each with a distinctly different way of arriving at his number. Each may use a *time-weighted* rate of return formula, but their presentations may be so different that comparisons are impossible.

Also, some managers were advertising their performance results in newspapers. Given the lack of standards, there was potential for inconsistency and misrepresentation. The SEC hinted that they might establish some rules regarding the advertising of private account performance. Seeing these problems, the Financial Analysts Federation (FAF) formed a committee in 1986 to address the *reporting* of performance results (as did the ICAA, as noted previously).

It's interesting to contrast the FAF's efforts with those of the BAI. The BAI saw that there was quite a variety of ways firms were *calculating* rates of return and came up with a standard method. The FAF was aware that although firms might *calculate* returns in a similar way, the way they *reported* their numbers could vary significantly.

In 1990, the FAF joined with the ICFA (Institute of Chartered Financial Analysts) to form the Association for Investment Management & Research (AIMR). AIMR picked up the ball from the FAF to come up with reporting standards.

In 1993, the AIMR published their *Performance Presentation Standards* which, for the first time, detailed how managers should report performance to prospective clients. AIMR's goal was to establish a *level playing field* so that each manager's numbers could be properly judged relative to her competition and so that plan sponsors could effectively assess how managers perform.

Composites—the Basis for the AIMR Standards

The main concept proposed by the AIMR standards is the creation of *composites*. A composite is a group of accounts with similar investment styles and objectives. This concept ties back to the BAI's recommendation that accounts be classified for better comparison.

AIMR requires that *all fee-paying, fully discretionary accounts* be included in at least one composite. Firms wishing to comply with the AIMR standards must come up with the composites they'll use to promote their business. Composites tend to be based heavily on investment style, but other characteristics can also come into play, such as account type (e.g., Taft-Hartley), tax status, and restrictions.

The firm must review its accounts to determine which composite(s) an account should belong to. It's quite common to find some *oddball* accounts that don't seem to *fit* into one of the defined composites. In this case, the manager should group *similar* accounts and create new composites. In cases where there is only one account with a particular style or characteristic, *single account composites* can be formed. To comply with AIMR's standards, the use of a *catch-all, garbage,* or *dustbin* composite is not permitted.

Discretion

One of the areas of flexibility is in the use of the term *discretion*. There are so many ways to interpret discretion that AIMR didn't want to dictate when an account *is* or *is not* discretionary.

There are some obvious cases when all or most managers would agree that an account is nondiscretionary—for example, when an account requires that the manager receive the account's authorization before any transaction is executed. Beyond this, the situation is often open to interpretation.

For example, some clients place category restrictions on their accounts (e.g., no *sin stocks,* no *South African stocks,* no *stocks that don't employ union workers*). Others may restrict the purchase of certain securities (e.g., an executive at a public company may be entitled to stock options and would not benefit from a manager purchasing shares in his company).

In these cases, some managers will feel that the restrictions are such that they have to classify the account as nondiscretionary, while other managers won't feel this need. Some managers may create separate composites that have similar restrictions, so that the accounts can be included.

Chapter 9 goes into greater detail on the AIMR standards. Suffice it to say that AIMR's efforts have become widely accepted. A 1995 survey by The Spaulding Group revealed that over 90% of money management firms either comply or plan to comply with the standards.[8] In addition, many non-US firms are adopting presentation standards, so as to *level the playing field* between managers seeking new clients.

INVESTMENT MANAGEMENT CONSULTANTS' ASSOCIATION

AIMR isn't the only U.S.-based organization to offer performance presentation standards. The Investment Management Consultants' Association (IMCA) also published *The Consultants' Performance Standards* in 1993 to define a proper and consistent reporting methodology.

Although the IMCA standards are actually geared to pension fund consultants, because of the fact that these consultants normally don't present performance results but rather call upon money managers to do so, the standards end up being directed to money managers. The IMCA standards are very similar to AIMR's, with the main exception being the requirement for *equal-weighted* rather than *asset-weighted* composites.[9]

The 1995 Spaulding Group surveys found little acceptance for the IMCA standards among either money managers, pension fund consultants, or verification firms.[10] In reality, many firms that comply with AIMR can also easily comply with IMCA, since the main difference is the *weighting* of composites. Consultants will often ask for *equal-weighted* returns, even though they're not aware this is an IMCA standard.

CHAPTER SUMMARY

As a result of the BAI, ICAA, AIMR, and IMCA, the money management industry now has performance measurement standards that define proper, accurate, and consistent ways to calculate and present performance results. Most firms recognize the advantages and benefits of complying with all or most of these standards, for calculating account-level and composite-level rates of return.

The international investing community is also adopting presentation standards. AIMR has a global standards subcommittee that's working with various international organizations to help formulate standards. Several countries have adopted standards similar to AIMR's while others are exploring this matter.

ENDNOTES

1. S. C. Bernstein [date unknown], p. 6.
2. S. C. Bernstein [date unknown], p. 4.
3. Arthur Stedry Hansen Consulting Actuaries, "Measurement of Trust Performance." Unpublished report submitted to NABAC, 1966.
4. BAI [1968], page 3.
5. Ibid., p. 4.
6. Advisers that are not affiliated with brokers, insurance companies, or banks.
7. Transaction costs include commissions, fees (e.g., SEC fees, ticket charges), market impact, and other factors relating to getting an order executed by a broker.
8. TSG [1995], p. 3.
9. An equal-weighted composite return is simply the basic arithmetic mean, while an asset-weighted composite return weights each participant's contribution to the overall average based on the beginning period market value.
10. Only 30% of the money managers surveyed claimed to (or indicated plans to) comply with the IMCA standards. Almost 35% of the money managers surveyed weren't even familiar with the IMCA standards. While 80% of the consultants surveyed *always* inquire into a firm's compliance with AIMR, the remainder *often* or *sometimes* inquire. Only 10% *always* ask about compliance with IMCA, and 16.7% *often* or *sometimes* pursue this information.

CHAPTER 9

The AIMR Standards

As noted in chapter 8, the Association for Investment Management & Research (AIMR) has published standards for the presentation of performance results. These standards have been widely accepted by the industry, but many firms are still trying to comply. The AIMR standards stress performance *presentation* rather than calculation. They allow some flexibility regarding calculations within certain boundaries. In this chapter, we'll discuss some ideas about how a firm can go about complying with the standards.

A COMMON MISCONCEPTION

One of the most common misconceptions is that a firm is *in compliance* if their portfolio accounting or performance system vendor is *in compliance*. This misconception was partly fostered by aggressive advertising on the part of some industry software vendors.

The reality is that software *can't* comply with the standards. Software is a *tool* that helps the *firm* comply with the AIMR standards. While this tool is extremely important, it's only part of the process. As you'll see from the information that follows, there are numerous tasks that must be performed.

Another misconception is that individual composites can be in compliance rather than the whole firm. This is incorrect. While AIMR allows a firm to have individual composites verified (see below), the firm must be in compliance with the standards.

SHOULD YOU COMPLY?

The first step in becoming compliant is to have some reason for complying. The AIMR-PPS is voluntary, so why should a firm spend the time and money adhering to voluntary standards? Recent survey results[1] disclosed the following reasons for firms complying with the standards:

a.	Member of AIMR	60.2%[2]
b.	Marketing advantage of being compliant	81.4%
c.	Pressure from clients	8.8%
d.	Pressure from [investment] consultants	33.6%
e.	Pressure from prospects	17.7%
f.	SEC position relative to the standards	32.7%[3]
g.	Other	6.2%

Membership in AIMR is sufficient grounds for complying, since AIMR members are obligated to adhere to AIMR guidelines.

It's very common for a firm's marketing department to encourage compliance, due to the increasing demand from prospects and investment consultants. Marketing clearly sees an advantage in complying with the standards.

FORMING A TASK FORCE

Complying with AIMR's standards isn't a one-person job, nor is it something that can be done easily or quickly. A task force should be formed with representatives from the following areas of the firm:

1. Marketing. Most firms choose to comply with the AIMR standards based on the perceived marketing advantage compliance will bring.[4] Therefore, it's important that marketing participate. Composites should be geared to the de-

mands of the marketplace, to ensure that the reported numbers match up with a prospect's objectives. Marketing
should know best what the market looks like. Their input is
very important in this process.

2. Portfolio Management. Portfolio managers *know* how
they're investing client assets. They also know under what
circumstances an account is *discretionary* and when it isn't.
There are many aspects of compliance that call for input
from this group.

3. Back Office Operations. This is the area that's typically
charged with maintaining client portfolios, calculating performance results, and publishing reports. This group is
often charged with the responsibility of creating and maintaining a firm's composites. It's important, therefore, that
this group participate in any discussions regarding AIMR
compliance.

In addition, there will be times when input from the systems
department will be necessary. Changes to a firm's portfolio accounting and/or performance system may be needed to provide
the needed functionality for AIMR compliance.

DEFINING COMPOSITES

One of the first steps in complying with AIMR is to define the
composites the firm will create. A composite is a collection or
grouping of accounts (or portions of accounts) with similar characteristics (e.g., they should have the same investment style, objective, or strategy; they may also be of the same type [e.g., taxable ac-
counts] or have other common characteristics [e.g., same
investment type]). Composites should match up with client objectives and investment styles. Firms may find that a single style may
have variations. For example, there may be a basic *large cap* composite. In addition, there may be one for clients that have *restrictions,* and another for *taxable accounts.* TSG's survey found the average number of composites to be 20, with a high of 415. This high
is clearly an exception, but it isn't unusual to find larger firms with
50 or more composites, especially if they offer a large variety of investment styles.

Firms also have the option of creating asset-level composites (e.g., equity) that can include the asset portion of a balanced account. If this is to be done, not only that asset's return but the cash portion of the asset must also be included. Therefore, it's important that the *method* for allocating cash be determined. Alternative methods of allocating cash are described in chapter 3.

CALCULATING COMPOSITE RETURNS

AIMR requires that composite returns be asset-weighted. They also recommend that equal-weighted composite returns be calculated.[5] There are three methods of deriving asset-weighted composites.

Weight by Beginning Period Market Values

The first method (and probably the most common) is to weight by the beginning period market value.[6]

Table 9–1 shows an example of how to calculate both the equal and asset-weighted return. We've shown ten accounts with varying market values and rates of return. The beginning period market value is multiplied by the rate of return (in decimal format) to de-

T A B L E   9–1

Asset-Weighted ROR

Account	Beginning Period Market Value	ROR	Account Weighted ROR
A	100,000	2%	2,000
B	120,000	1.5%	1,800
C	140,000	3%	4,200
D	160,000	2.5%	4,000
E	180,000	4%	7,200
F	200,000	2.5%	5,000
G	220,000	3%	6,600
H	240,000	2%	4,800
I	260,000	1.5%	3,900
J	280,000	1%	2,800
Totals	1,900,000		42,300
		2.3%	2.23%

rive each account's weighted ROR. We sum both the beginning period market values and the account weighted RORs. Mathematically this method is shown as:

$$Asset\text{-}Weighted\ ROR = \frac{\sum\limits_{i=1}^{n} BMV_i \cdot ROR_i}{\sum\limits_{i=1}^{n} BMV_i}$$

$$= \frac{(100{,}000 \cdot 0.02) + (120{,}000 \cdot 0.015) + (140{,}000 \cdot 0.03) + \ldots +}{(100{,}000 + 120{,}000 + 140{,}000 + \ldots + 280{,}000)}$$

$$= \frac{42{,}300}{1{,}900{,}000} = 2.23\%$$

The asset-weighted ROR is found to be 2.23 percent.

This table also shows the equal-weighted ROR for this composite (2.3%). It's derived by summing the rates of return and dividing by the number of items in the composite. Mathematically:

$$Equal\text{-}Weighted\ ROR = \frac{\sum\limits_{i=1}^{n} ROR_i}{n}$$

Weight by Beginning Period Market Values Plus Cash Flows

The second approach is similar to the first. In addition to market values, we include intraperiod cash flows (i.e., any contributions or withdrawals that occur during the period). Some people feel this is an improvement over the first method, since it takes into consideration large flows.

These flows should be day-weighted to reflect the amount of time they were in or out of the composite. The formula we introduced in chapter 2 can be used for this purpose:

$$W_i = \frac{CD - D_i}{CD}$$

where

W_i = the proportion of the total number of days in the period
the cash flow has been in (or out) of the portfolio
CD = the total number of calendar days in the period
D = the total number of days since the beginning of the
period in which the cash flow F_i occurred

So if the measurement period is the month of June (30 days),
and the flow occurred on the 5th, the formula becomes

$$W_i = \frac{30 - 5}{30} = \frac{25}{30} = 0.833$$

meaning that the money was in (or out of) the account 83.3% of the
time.

The formula for deriving the asset-weighted-plus-cash-flow
ROR is as follows:

$$Asset\text{-}Weighted\text{-}Plus\text{-}Cash\text{-}Flow\ ROR = \frac{\sum\limits_{i=1}^{n}(BMV_i + \sum\limits_{j=1}^{m}CF_{i,j} \cdot WD_{i,j}) \cdot ROR_i}{\sum\limits_{i=1}^{n}(BMV_i + \sum\limits_{j=1}^{m}CF_{i,j} \cdot WD_{i,j})}$$

Table 9–2 shows an example of how to employ this formula.

In our example, the asset-weighted-plus-cash-flows ROR
(2.21%) is only slightly different from the asset-weighted return
(2.23%). The number and magnitude of the cash flows will affect
the composite's return.

Aggregate Return

This approach treats the composite as if it were a single portfolio.
Table 9–3 continues our earlier example. Here, we sum the beginning market values and ending market values. The cash flows are
treated as if they took place for this aggregate account. We'll use
the Dietz asset-weighted formula from chapter 2.

$$R = \left(\frac{EMV - (1 - WD) \cdot C}{BMV + WD \cdot C} - 1 \right) \cdot 100$$

$$= \left(\frac{\begin{matrix} 1{,}991{,}645 - ((1 - 0.667) \cdot 9{,}000) - ((1 - 0.500) \cdot 55{,}000) \\ - ((1 - 0.33) \cdot (-15{,}000)) - 1) \cdot 100 \end{matrix}}{\begin{matrix} 1{,}900{,}000 + (0.667 \cdot 9{,}000) + \\ (0.500 \cdot 55{,}000) + (0.333 \cdot (-15{,}000)) \end{matrix}} - 1 \right) \cdot 100$$

T A B L E   9–2

Asset-Weighted-Plus-Cash-Flows ROR

Acc't	BMV	Cash Flow/ Date of Flow	ROR	W_i	Account Weighted ROR
A	100,000	$9,000/10th	2%	(30 − 10)/30 = 0.667	0.02 * (100,000 + 9,000 * 0.667
		$5,000/15th		(30 − 15)/30 = 0.500	+ 5,000 * 0.5) = 2,170
B	120,000	−$15,000/20th	1.5%	(30 − 20)/30 = 0.333	0.015 * (120,000— 15,000 * 0.333) = 1,725
C	140,000		3%		0.03 * 140,000 = 4,200
D	160,000		2.5%		4,000
E	180,000		4%		7,200
F	200,000		2.5%		5,000
G	220,000		3%		6,600
H	240,000		2%		4,800
I	260,000		1.5%		3,900
J	280,000	$50,000/15th	1%	(30−15)/30 = 0.500	0.01 * (280,000 + 50,000 * 0.5) = 3,050
	1,900,000	Total Weighted Flows = 6,000 + 2,500—5,000 + 25,000 = 28,500			Total Account Weighted ROR = 42,645
		Total of Market Values Plus Weighted Flows = 1,900 + 28,500 = 1,928,500			Asset-Weighted- Plus-Cash-Flows ROR = 2.21%

$$= \left(\frac{1{,}991{,}645 - 3{,}000 - 27{,}500 - (-10{,}000)}{1{,}900{,}000 + 6{,}000 + 27{,}500 - 5000} - 1\right) \cdot 100$$

$$= \left(\frac{1{,}971{,}145}{1{,}928{,}500} - 1\right) \cdot 100 = (1.0221 - 1) \cdot 100 = 2.21\%$$

The results are in line with the first two methods.

   Regardless of which method a firm chooses to use, it should be consistent. An exception can be made for the second approach

T A B L E   9–3

Aggregate ROR

Acc't	BMV	Cash Flow/ Date of Flow	W$_i$	ROR	EMV
A	100,000	$9,000/10th	(30 – 10)/30 = 0.667	2%	116,170
		$5,000/15th	(30 – 15)/30 = 0.500		
B	120,000	–$15,000/20th	(30 – 20)/30 = 0.333	1.5%	106,725
C	140,000			3%	144,200
D	160,000			2.5%	164,000
E	180,000			4%	187,200
F	200,000			2.5%	205,000
G	220,000			3%	226,600
H	240,000			2%	244,800
I	260,000			1.5%	263,900
J	280,000	$50,000/15th	(30 – 15)/30 = 0.500	1%	333,050
Totals	1,900,000	$9,000/10th	(30 – 10)/30 = 0.667	2.21%	1,991,645
		$55,000/15th	(30 – 15)/30 = 0.500		
		–$15,000/20th	(30 – 20)/30 = 0.33		

(asset-weighted-plus-cash flows). An argument can be made for using this on an exception basis (e.g., when cash flows exceed a certain percentage in any account), but this should be documented and employed consistently when these exceptions arise.

RETROACTIVE COMPLIANCE

Firms need to decide how far back they will comply. One common misconception is that a firm only needs to comply as of the date they get their records in order, since the 1993 AIMR standards report *recommended* but didn't *require* retroactive compliance.[7] However, this is for periods *prior to January 1, 1993.* To comply with the standards, a firm must have their performance results in compliance at least back till January 1993 (January 1994 for taxable accounts) or to the firm's inception, if later. Here's the unattractive rule: If a firm *can't* comply back this far, but can get their numbers in order as of a later date, they won't be able to claim compliance until *ten years* after this date! One reason it's necessary to decide how far back a firm will comply is that *all* accounts managed during this period must be reviewed for compliance, not just the ones that are still active.

Here's an example that should make this rule clearer. Firm "A" made the decision to comply with the AIMR standards before they went into effect in January 1993.[8] Firm "A" has been in existence since 1980. In reviewing the draft standards, they decided to comply retroactively for 10 years (i.e., back to 1983). Several of the firm's employees spent long hours in the summer and fall of 1992 going through their files, retrieving historical records for both active and inactive accounts, deciding what composites to have and which accounts would go into which ones, reviewing their computer system's capabilities and making the necessary changes to provide the appropriate functionality, calculating asset-weighted returns, and preparing the appropriate disclosure documents. By the end of 1992, they were confident that the past 10 years' figures were "in compliance" with the AIMR-PPS, and were prepared to continue to comply going forward.

Firm "B" has also been in existence since 1980. They, too, wanted to comply with the new AIMR standards, but didn't have the time or resources to go through all their records to comply retroactively. So they decided in 1992 to come into compliance as of January 1993. They spent time in 1992 reviewing their various management styles and strategies in order to decide which composites to construct. They also decided which accounts should go into which composites. And they made sure that their portfolio accounting vendor would have the appropriate functionality in the performance system to allow them to comply going forward from January 1993. Effective that month, they believed they were complying. As part of their marketing materials, they provided 10 years' worth of returns, but indicated that these numbers didn't comply with the AIMR standards and specified the reasons why.

Firm "C," too, has been managing money since 1980. In 1992, their management wasn't sure they wanted to bother with the AIMR standards. They knew a lot of work would be involved and weren't sure they wanted to spend the time or money, so they decided to wait. In 1995, they obtained a copy of the results of a survey[9] that revealed that over 75% of the firms that participated claimed compliance and another 15% planned to comply. They also learned that most investment consulting firms were asking about AIMR compliance as part of their search process. They had been noticing that more and more Requests for Proposals were asking them to indicate whether or not they were in compliance. The firm's marketing staff had been urging the firm to comply, and management finally made the decision to do so.

In reviewing the AIMR standards, they noticed that "retroactive compliance is recommended but not required."[10] Rather than take the time and effort to create compliant performance figures back to January 1993, they decided that starting January 1, 1996, they would begin to comply. They spent time in 1995 reviewing their investment styles and client characteristics, creating composites, and getting organized. They were prepared to provide prospective clients with 10 years' worth of historical returns, with the appropriate disclosures as to why these figures weren't in compliance with the AIMR-PPS. Their portfolio accounting vendor had long ago enhanced its performance module so that it had the appropriate functionality and features to support AIMR compliance, so they were confident that beginning in January 1996 they could claim compliance.

Unfortunately, Firm "C" has a problem. While retroactive compliance is technically only a recommendation, that is as of January 1993 (i.e., retroactive means going back from January 1993). For purposes of AIMR compliance after that date, the firm must get its numbers into compliance back at least through 1993 in order to claim compliance. Since Firm "C" hasn't done this, they won't be able to claim compliance for 10 years, or until the year 2006.

Some firms aren't able to create compliant numbers because their records have been lost or destroyed. AIMR has made a provision for this. Take the case of Firm "D." This advisory firm was formed in 1990. In June 1995, they had a fire that destroyed all their records, including performance results. They are not able to re-create these records, but they can still claim compliance as of July 1995. They must, however, disclose that even though the firm has been in existence since 1990, historical records were destroyed and cannot be re-created.

This has been a somewhat lengthy discussion on the term *retroactive.* Hopefully the examples clarify what the term means relative to AIMR-PPS compliance.

DEFINE-DISCRETIONARY RULES

The firm must decide under what circumstances an account will be called *nondiscretionary.* AIMR is fairly flexible in this regard, so the burden falls on the firm to make this decision. There may be some clear-cut cases (e.g., those accounts that require approval of trades before they're exercised) but there may also be some that aren't so clear.

For example, what restrictions have been placed on the firm? Do these really impact the manager's ability to invest? Are there enough accounts with similar restrictions to warrant the creation of a *composite with restrictions?* This may be appropriate if the firm typically markets to prospects with these restrictions.

Do *directed brokerage* requirements place an unwieldy impediment on the manager's ability to obtain good performance? This, too, may cause the firm to develop a *composite with direction,* since more and more institutional accounts direct some or all their commission dollars.

REVIEWING CLIENT ACCOUNTS

Each account needs to be reviewed to decide what composite(s) it should be placed in. This can be a very nontrivial exercise. As noted above, all accounts that have been managed during the period must be reviewed, even those that are no longer active.

Accounts should be reviewed for the following:

1. Discretionary versus Non-discretionary. Using the rules the firm's defined, decide if an account is discretionary or not. There may have been times in the account's life that it *was* nondiscretionary. This is acceptable. At such times, the account would be removed from the composite.

2. Composite Membership. What composite(s) should the account belong to? Has the account's investment style changed over time, which might warrant the account going from one composite to another?

   Is the account's style inconsistent with others? If so, the firm may elect to create *single-account composites*. Many firms have elected to create *catch-all* or *garbage* composites, to group those accounts that don't match up with the firm's other composites. Although this practice is somewhat common, it's a violation of the AIMR standards and should be avoided.[11]

3. Fee-based. The AIMR standards require the inclusion of accounts that pay advisory fees into composites. Non-fee-paying accounts may be included, but this must be disclosed.

DATA AVAILABILITY

The firm must determine the availability of the necessary data to support compliance. The following are needed, on at least a quarterly basis:

- account-level time-weighted rates of return (with the proper accruing of income)
- advisory fees paid (if *net-of-fee* performance will be reported)
- account-level beginning of period market values
- asset-level rates of return[12]

In some cases, these data may be available only in *hard copy* format. In these cases, a lot of work will be necessary to get the data into an automated format.

In other cases, the data may exist on the computer, which will obviously make the job easier. Often, the firm has changed systems, which may require data conversion. This will often necessitate a fairly detailed review of file definitions and the development of computer programs to map the data from the old format to a new one.

Some effort is typically needed to get account-level data into the firm's composite creation and reporting system. A plan should be prepared, with input from the back office and systems, and possibly the firm's software vendor, to decide how data will be provided for the firm's composites.

PRESENTATION CONTENT AND FORMAT

The AIMR standards are *presentation* standards. The firm needs to decide how it will present its AIMR-compliant information to prospective clients.

While AIMR goes into some detail regarding the required disclosures and data requirements, the specific format is up to each firm. Also, AIMR allows for supplemental information that a firm may feel highlights their performance.

MEASURES OF DISPERSION

The 1996 AIMR standards book requires the use of a dispersion value (e.g., high-low, standard deviation). AIMR does not recognize any method for "linking" subperiod standard deviation values to arrive at a longer period value (i.e., under AIMR guidelines, you can't take the standard deviations for January, February, and March to arrive at the standard deviation for the first quarter). As a result, the only portfolios that can be used in the calculation of a standard deviation are those that were present the full period. To be more specific, if you're calculating the standard deviation for a full year, the only account annual returns that would go into the formula would be those that were present the full year. While this can be a challenge for firms that experience a lot of volatility in their composites, it's a guideline that must be adhered to.

AIMR suggests an alternative dispersion measure: asset-weighted standard deviation:[13]

$$S_c = \sqrt{\sum W_i \cdot [R_i - WtMEAN(R)]^2}$$

$$w_i = \frac{BMV_i}{\sum BMV_i}$$

where

$$WtMEAN = \frac{\sum BMV_i\,(R_i)}{\sum BMV_i}$$

The value, W_i is the weight of the ith portfolio in the composite. The weighted-mean formula ($WtMEAN$) is similar to the formula shown for finding the asset-weighted return for the composite. Its denominator emphasizes that only the market values for those accounts present for the full period will be included.

We'll use the data from Table 9–1 as an example of how to calculate this value. All the accounts were present for the full period, so the weighted mean is 2.23 percent. Table 9–4 gives the results for deriving the asset-weighted standard deviation. We find the value to be 0.008729, or 0.8729 percent. The standard deviation for this composite is 0.8426%, slightly lower than the weighted version.

VERIFICATION

Verification is a process used to ensure that a firm who *thinks* they're complying with the AIMR-PPS actually *is*. AIMR doesn't require verification, but rather recommends it. AIMR has established some guidelines for this process.[14] One of the most important is that the exercise be done by an independent, objective third party (i.e., not by the firm themselves or an affiliate of the firm).

There are two "levels" of verification. Level One is sometimes referred to as *firm-wide* verification. Here, the *verifier* would check to make sure the firm is complying with the rules. For example:

- that all fee-paying, fully discretionary accounts are in at least one composite
- that a list of all composites is available to prospective clients
- that such accounts that aren't in composites are excluded for legitimate reasons (e.g., they are below a particular asset level)
- that the firm is employing a proper method for calculating composite returns
- that disclosure materials are in accordance with AIMR guidelines
- that all rules are properly adhered to (e.g., that the firm hasn't established a *catch-all* or *dustbin* composite for portfolios that don't easily fit in with other composites)

AIMR's Level Two verification is more like an audit. It can be done at the composite level. AIMR will permit a Level Two to be done, providing a Level One is done *at least for* the composite(s)

T A B L E 9–4

Example: Asset-Weighted Standard Deviation

Account	Beginning Period Market Value (BMV)	ROR (R)	Account Weighted ROR (BMV_i (R_i))	R_i – WtMEAN(R)	$[R_i - \text{WtMEAN(R)}]^2$	w_i	w_i $[R_i - \text{WtMEAN(R)}]^2$
A	100,000		2,000	-0.23%	0.000005	0.0526	0.00000028
B	120,000	1.5%	1,800	-0.73%	0.000053	0.0632	0.00000337
C	140,000	3%	4,200	0.77%	0.000059	0.0737	0.00000437
D	160,000	2.5%	4,000	0.27%	0.000007	0.0842	0.00000061
E	180,000	4%	7,200	1.77%	0.000313	0.0947	0.00002968
F	200,000	2.5%	5,000	0.27%	0.000007	0.0153	0.00000077
G	220,000	3%	6,600	0.775%	0.000059	0.1158	0.00000687
H	240,000	2%	4,800	-0.23%	0.000005	0.1263	0.00000067
I	260,000	1.5%	3,900	-0.73%	0.000053	0.1368	0.00000729
J	280,000	1%	2,800	-1.23%	0.000151	0.1474	0.00002230
Totals	1,900,000		Σ BMV$_i$ = 42,300				0.00007620

WtMEAN(R) = 2.23%

Weighted Std Dev =
0.008729
or 0.8729%

that are undergoing the Level Two. That is, a verifier would make sure that all the accounts that *should* be in the composite being verified *are*, and that there are no accounts present that shouldn't be. Also, that the calculations and disclosures are proper and complete for that composite.

The Level Two (or audit) part goes into greater detail. The verifier will check pricing, validate account holdings (by comparing the firm's records with the custodian's), transactions (including income), and account-level rates of return. Firms wishing to have a Level Two performed *must* be in compliance with the AIMR-PPS entirely, not just for the composite(s) being verified.

Before undergoing a verification, the firm should have some level of confidence that they are, indeed, in compliance. Otherwise, the exercise can be quite costly and time-consuming.

The Spaulding Group's 1995 Performance Survey found that, on average, verification firms expected only 57% of companies requesting a verification to actually be in compliance with the AIMR-PPS.[15] This means that 43% of the firms requesting to be verified, who actually believe the are in compliance, actually aren't. This strongly suggests the need for verification, since a firm holding themselves out as being in compliance with the AIMR-PPS but who actually aren't complying can be charged with fraud—something most firms wouldn't welcome.

I occasionally encounter situations where firms truly believe they're complying, but for one reason or another they are falling short of the mark. One particular occasion is worth noting. I attended a conference dealing with the AIMR standards. One of the sessions involved a panel discussion on three firms' experiences in coming into compliance. One of the speakers explained that they hadn't undergone verification (due to the cost involved). He discussed the rationale behind their decision to comply and the process they undertook. In the course of his presentation, he shared enough information with the audience for me to determine that they were probably not in compliance (he explained that they had constructed a "catch-all" composite for those accounts that didn't fit into any of their standard composites; this is a violation of the AIMR-PPS). This example reinforces the importance of verification.[16]

CAN'T BE IN "PARTIAL" COMPLIANCE

Some firms will state that they "comply with the AIMR-PPS, with the exception ..." This is incorrect. You either *are* in compliance or *not*. You can't be partially in compliance with the standards.

CHAPTER SUMMARY

AIMR has made a tremendous impact on the investment community, not just in the U.S. but throughout the world. The AIMR-PPS provides the foundation for an ethical representation of a firm's performance results to prospective clients. The standards provide a level playing field to improve competition, not just for the money managers but also for their prospective customers. They're nontrivial and often require a great deal of effort to understand and apply. We've discussed many of the key aspects of the standards and how a firm should go about complying with them. One of these is the creation and maintenance of composites, which should represent the firm's various management styles and characteristics. Decisions regarding composite creation should involve a great deal of thought and analysis. The AIMR-PPS are achieving the goals they were originally established for, and I fully support them and strongly recommend compliance with them. Appendix A provides additional details regarding these very important standards.

ENDNOTES

1. TSG [1995], p. 3.
2. Results will exceed 100% because respondees were permitted to choose more than one answer.
3. Although the SEC does not endorse these standards, they have shown support for them.
4. 81.4% of the respondents to The Spaulding Group survey cited *marketing advantage of being compliant* as the motivating reason for complying with AIMR's standards. This was the number one answer given. TSG [1995], p. 3.
5. In reality, firms are forced to do both, since many investment consultants and plan sponsors require such calculations when they're searching for a manager.
6. This is one of the areas of confusion with the standards. The beginning period market value is normally the ending value for the preceding period, so some firms have erroneously used the ending period market values. The problem with this is that the ending period values reflect the performance that occurred during the period (i.e.,

accounts that appreciated will contribute more to the return than those that depreci-ated in value). The market values at the beginning of the measurement period, be it a month or quarter, are to be used.

7. "For periods prior to January 1, 1993, a firm has the option of restating historical per-formance numbers in accordance with the standards." AIMR [1993], p. 2.

8. For this example, we'll assume that all three of these firms are managing nontaxable ac-counts and are therefore subject to that January 1, 1993, compliance date. January 1, 1994, deals with taxable accounts.

9. "Performance Measurement Surveys, Summary Results," June 1995, conducted and published by The Spaulding Group, Inc.

10. "Performance Presentation Standards, 1993," published by AIMR, p. 7.

11. AIMR [1996], p. 29.

12. This is necessary only if the firm will extract the asset-level return portion of a balanced account with a single asset class composite.

13. AIMR [1996], p. 98. (Please note: The formula depicted in the revised standards has er-rors. Please refer to AIMR [1993], page 40).

14. AIMR [1996], pp. 103–113.

15. TSG [1995], p. 21.

16. I make this recommendation without any conflict of interest, since my firm doesn't pro-vide verification services. Because of my years of experience with the standards and my numerous encounters with various money management firms, I've come to real-ize that there's a great deal of confusion and misunderstanding about the standards. Having a knowledgeable third-party review a firm's operation, documentation, pro-cedures, and disclosures should provide a firm with confidence in their claims of compliance, and avoid problems in the event they really aren't complying.

CHAPTER 10

Benchmarks: Comparing the Firm's Performance

Measuring something has little meaning unless we have something to compare the value against. In general, by itself, a firm's rate of return number has little meaning.[1] If I tell you that my performance last year was 18.2%, will you be impressed or concerned?

To be meaningful, we need something to compare the return to. There are generally two comparative measures that are used to tell us whether the return is good or bad: benchmarks and peer groups. This chapter will address these, as well as a relatively new concept, portfolio opportunity distributions (PODs), as viable methods of comparing performance.

INDEXES

The most common benchmarks are indexes. Most institutional assets are managed against an index, sometimes called the "bogey."

Indexes are values that are based on the performance of a group of underlying securities. For example, the Standard & Poor's 500 (or S&P 500) is made up of 500 securities that trade on the New York Stock Exchange (NYSE). Each day, these 500 securities are priced. If we treat this group as a portfolio, we can measure its performance from one period to the next, and this is what is done when we compare a manager's return to it—we measure the performance of the index from one period to the next and see how our performance compares.

Indexes are used to measure the value added by the manager. If the fund's objective was to equal the index, then a passive, or index, manager should be employed. However, if the fund is interested in *beating* the index, then an active manager is selected. His investment skill contributes to his success (or failure) in beating the index.

Constructing an Index

When an index provider is building an index, she needs to decide what she's attempting to measure. For example, it can be a broad market index, covering a mix of companies (such as the S&P 500); an industry-specific index (e.g., the technology sector); an index that's targeted to a capitalization segment; an index that's comprised of bonds with a particular maturity period; or an index that's targeted to a global segment (e.g., emerging markets). Next, the provider needs to identify the pool of candidate participants— that is, what stocks or bonds are available to choose from.

Of 100% of these candidates, the provider needs to decide how many she'll use and the criteria she'll employ to make this selection. Of the universe of securities available, what percentage will be used? For example, in picking a country to include in an emerging market index, how many of the available companies will be selected?

With an international or global index, the provider needs to decide what proportion each country will represent and what countries to include. One common type of global index is the EAFE (Europe, Australia, Far East) variety. Here, it's typical that the mix of countries will be based on each country's gross national product or its total market capitalization. A shortcoming is the major role Japan would play; therefore, another index EAFE, ex Japan, has emerged as an alternative.

The index may *equal weight* the representation of each of the underlying securities or may *market cap weight* the participants, giving heavier weighting to the larger companies in the index. An alternative weighting scheme is *price weighting*, where each security's market price is used to determine its portion of the index, where heavier weightings are given to those securities with higher market prices. Knowing the method an index provider used to construct an index can be quite valuable in deciding how valid the index is for comparing the firm's portfolio's returns.

In deciding the portion a country will represent, it's important to consider what restrictions the country may have placed on foreign ownership. Many countries limit the amount of their corporations a foreigner can purchase. This restriction should be considered when constructing an index, so that the index doesn't represent a situation that has no basis in reality (i.e., that can't be achieved because of the restrictions).

Picking the Right Index

Having something to compare a return against is only valuable if the thing we're using has some relevance. For example, to compare a bond portfolio against the S&P 500 would be unreasonable, since the S&P 500 is made up exclusively of stocks and our portfolio only has fixed-income securities. It would also be unreasonable to compare a stock portfolio against the S&P 500 if that portfolio was comprised of low capitalization stocks that only trade over-the-counter. Ideally, we want to compare *apples to apples*.

INDEX WEIGHTING SCHEMES[2]

- Capitalization-Weighted
  - Heavier weighting to larger names
  - Self-rebalancing
  - Ideally should be float-weighted
- Equal-Weighted
  - All securities or countries have same weight
  - Involves transactions due to rebalancing
  - Small stocks/countries have heavy weighting
- GDP- (Gross Domestic Product) Weighted
  - Weight countries by their economic output
  - Weighed to adjust for different valuations
  - Involves transactions due to rebalancing

At one time, the industry relied on just a few indexes for comparison purposes. But as our portfolios have grown in complexity and mix, these few indexes simply haven't been adequate. The ongoing globalization of portfolios—especially into *emerging markets*—only emphasizes the need for more indexes.

Today, there are literally thousands of indexes available to choose from. Various index providers[3] often offer competing benchmarks for the same industry segment. Firms have to decide which index best matches their investment style or portfolio makeup.

Clients often make this decision as part of their contract with the money manager. They may establish one or more indexes and set performance goals *vis-à-vis* these indexes. The manager must agree that these indexes are valid ones to use in comparing their performance.

Attributes of a good index include the following:[4]

Objective: The index should be identified ahead of time, it should be easily understood, and the construction rules should be clearly defined.

Replicable: The manager should be able to replicate the returns passively.

Investable: The manager should be able to "buy" the index.

Relevant: The index should represent the manager's "neutral" position.

U.S. domestic indexes can usually achieve these attributes. However, non-U.S. indexes may not. For example, some *third-world countries* place restrictions on the amount of stock an outsider may own. Unless the index takes these constraints into consideration, the resulting benchmark may not be achievable by a manager. Its relevance is then called into question.

Blending Indexes

Often, a firm won't be able to identify a single index that would suitably serve as a comparison tool. A good example is balanced accounts. Balanced accounts are made up of two or more security types (e.g., stock and bonds). The mix or ratio of stocks and bonds can vary. In these cases, many firms will provide two indexes for comparison—a stock index and a bond index. However, a customer would have a difficult time determining whether the manager's performance was good simply by comparing these two numbers. For example:

Portfolio A	18.2%
S&P 500	29.5%
Corporate Bond Index	7.8%

So, how did our manager perform? It's clear that his performance was superior to the bond index, but he didn't fare too well against the stock index. What's needed is a *blended* index for comparison purposes. The blend is a mix of the two indexes, based on the ratio of stocks and bonds in the portfolio. If the ratio is 50/50, we would take 50% of the stock index and add it to 50% of the bond index, yielding a benchmark that serves as a much better comparison tool. We would then report:

Portfolio A	18.2%
S&P 500	26.6%
Corporate Bond Index	7.8%
Blend (50/50)	17.2%

We can now see that our manager beat the benchmark by 100 basis points (1%).

Custom Benchmarks

In spite of the fact that there are thousands of benchmarks to choose from, some firms can't find one that adequately serves as a comparative tool. This is often the case when the client's objectives for the account include the funding of a liability schedule (e.g., a pension plan that must meet payment obligations). In these cases, a custom liability index may be in order. Certain index providers will construct custom indexes that properly serve this purpose.

Index Shortcomings

Indexes have several shortcomings that can make them less than ideal as comparative tools. First, they are typically reported *without income*. That is, they don't reflect any dividends or interest that may have been received during the measurement period. In some cases, a *with-income* index value is reported only monthly, while *without-income* values are the norm throughout the month. Since the manager's portfolios' performance is a *total return*, that is, *with* income, such a comparison would be less than fair, since the manager's performance has an advantage. If we know the underlying securities that make up the index, we can *derive* a *with-income* index on our own by determining the income that would have been received during the period.

By definition, an index can only contain what its name implies. A bond index may be comprised only of bonds, a stock index may hold only stocks. Yet each type receives income (interest and dividends), and it is important to understand how they treat this income. Some hold the cash until month-end or invest it in short-term cash equivalents. The proper step is to reinvest income back into the index.

Another shortcoming is that indexes don't reflect *transaction costs*. That is, no *buying* or *selling* occurs in the index, so there aren't any commissions or fees paid to acquire the securities. The manager's portfolio, on the other hand, reflects these added costs.

An increasingly important segment of the investment world is composed of the *passive,* or *index,* managers. Because many institutional investors are dissatisfied with their managers' ability to *beat* the index, they are willing to simply *buy* the index. That is, to have their portfolio yield the same return as the index. Unfortunately, *buying* the index won't yield the same return as the index because one has to pay transaction costs each time securities are purchased, so immediately upon making a purchase, one pays a cost that won't be reflected in the index.

While we know the makeup of the S&P 500, we don't know the makeup of all indexes, especially bond indexes. A *corporate bond index* may have one or many bonds, but we don't know how many or what they are.

Global indexes offer their own challenges. Now, we're introducing not just a mix of stocks, but also a mix of countries, where each country has its own economic factors. This is especially true with emerging-market indexes, where country variations can be significant. For example, one country's securities may have averaged an increase of over 100% during a year, while another's only yielded a return of less than 10%. The representation of one versus the other in the index can have a major impact on the index's overall return.

PEER GROUPS

Another benchmark that's often used is a peer group comparison—that is, the measurement of a manager against his or her peers. One of the challenges is to decide who the peers are. Often, managers are compared against the universe of money managers, most of whom manage against very different objectives. One example is the quarterly Investment Advisor's Equity Performance report, produced by Thomson Investment. This report compares all U.S. money managers who have submitted 13-F[5] reports to the SEC.

While this report's methodology can be criticized for a variety of reasons,[6] it provides a way to compare managers each quarter. However, the style differences from one manager to another aren't highlighted, nor is it possible to derive the various investment styles employed by a manager. Rather, a single number is used to represent a manager's performance.

When a firm is looking for a manager, they often define the *style* of manager they're looking for. Even though two managers may claim they use the same style, in actuality, there may be differences that suggest otherwise. This becomes evident when looking at certain reporting agencies' manager comparisons. For example, Lipper Analytical provides comparisons of mutual funds by style (growth, capital appreciation, etc.). When looking at the list of funds that comprise a particular style, it's not unusual to find fund names that don't match the style grouping. This is because the manager calls her fund one name, but Lipper feels the fund more properly belongs in a different category (based on their review of the fund's security position).

One challenge with peer group comparisons is survivorship bias. The firms that didn't do very well are no longer in business. Therefore, a manager is being compared against a group that has already outperformed other managers. Granted, all the managers in the group are suffering from this same disadvantage, but it's still worthwhile to consider the fact that the peer group is only made up of those peers that have succeeded (at least up to the date of comparison). Ron Surz offered a good analogy that highlights this problem.[7] If 1,000 runners start a marathon, but only 100 finish, is the 100th finisher in last place or in the top 10%?

Independent, third-party consultants are often the ones to produce peer group comparisons. Some do this on a continuing basis, taking in performance information from a group of managers each month or quarter. In other cases, the manager may solicit information on an *ad hoc* basis, to provide a client with information on which to base a manager selection decision.

There are many challenges with peer group comparisons. Since the managers are providing their numbers to the third-party consultants, we don't know how each manager's number was arrived at. Clearly, the AIMR Performance Presentation Standards provide some uniformity, but this is no guarantee that each manager is following the same approach when constructing his performance numbers. Also, we don't know the underlying securities that make up the reported returns. We also don't know what other factors contribute to a manager's performance (for example, if leverage was used or what rules he employs in defining discretion, for account inclusion/exclusion).

One way to achieve a more acceptable comparison of peers is for the manager and client or prospect to agree upon a universe of peers. Then, the third-party consultant can construct a peer universe that is a legitimate comparison for the manager to be measured against.

PORTFOLIO OPPORTUNITY DISTRIBUTIONS

A rather new concept in manager comparisons was developed by Ronald Surz—portfolio opportunity distributions. This is a topic he's written and spoken on extensively.[8]

In essence, this approach compares a manager against herself. That is, the manager defines the universe of possible holdings, based on whatever criteria she uses. From this universe, subsets of possible portfolios are constructed, and performance is measured for these subsets. Although hundreds or thousands of permutations are possible, construction is simplified because of the power of the computer. The result is essentially customized indexes that can serve as a benchmark for comparison against the manager's performance results.

Ron Surz feels that this approach eliminates the shortcomings of peer group and index comparisons. Only time will tell if the industry agrees, though he does offer an interesting alternative to consider.

CHAPTER SUMMARY

We've discussed the two most common methods of comparing rates of return: indexes and peer groups, and a new method, PODs, or portfolio opportunity distributions. Regardless of what measure is used, managers need to know how well they're doing relative to a valid comparative benchmark, and clients want to be able to compare, too. Otherwise, a return value is simply a number, with limited value.

ENDNOTES

1. As with anything, there are exceptions. Some clients have predefined a rate of return they want to realize on an annual basis. In these cases, as long as that goal is being met, they aren't concerned with what's happening elsewhere in the marketplace. But even in these cases, the number by itself has no meaning. It has to be compared with the return the client has defined. If the client's target is 15% and you've yielded 18.2%, you're 320 basis points (3.2%) above the target. If the requirement is 20%, then you're 180 basis points below.
2. Riddles, Neil [1996].
3. Index providers are often brokerage firms or financial data providers that perform the necessary calculations on a daily basis. They sell this data to distributors (e.g., quote services) and others to compensate for their costs.
4. Riddles, Neil [1996].
5. The 13-F is a quarterly report the SEC requires of any investment adviser who manages $100 million or more in equities or securities that are convertible into equities. The report lists the manager's holdings, by security, at the end of each calendar quarter.
6. At the beginning of each calendar quarter, Thomson takes the prior quarter's 13-F reports for each reporting manager and *assumes* that the holdings remained the same at the end of the period. The portfolio is priced using these *frozen* holdings and compared with the beginning period's value. This method doesn't take into consideration any transactions that have occurred during the intervening period. Nor does it include the effect of cash or other nonequity holdings. Nevertheless, the results are reported by various media each calendar quarter.
7. Surz [1994], page 38.
8. For example, see Surz [1994], and Surz [1996a], p. 38. Ron Surz also delivered presentations on PODs at the Institute for International Research's 1996 Performance Conferences (held in June and October 1996), chaired by the author.

CHAPTER 11

Policies, Procedures, Controls

The performance measurement process has always been an important one. However, with its increased focus, this importance has only grown further. We've also seen an increase in complexity, as information needs have expanded.

As with any complex process, it's important to establish the proper internal policies, procedures, and controls to ensure accuracy, completeness, and validity of the information that is reported.

POLICY/PROCEDURE MANUAL

Money management firms should develop documentation that outlines the firm's policies and the procedures necessary to carry them out.

A policy/procedure manual can ensure several things:

- Decisions about how things are to be done are thought about *before* they happen, when cooler heads prevail.
- When a problem occurs, people won't have to run around trying to get a decision made. The policy has already been established.
- When a problem recurs, the organization handles it in a manner consistent with previous occurrences.

I'll discuss a few examples of items that should be included in a policies/procedures manual.

PROCESSING ACCOUNT-LEVEL ADJUSTMENTS/CORRECTIONS

You've completed last month's report and then discover there was an error in the valuing of an account. Is the rate of return recalculated? What if there was a security pricing error that resulted in inaccurate returns being calculated? Or a cash flow that was missed? Or a trade that was processed for the wrong account? Or a trade that had to be canceled? These things happen all the time. How does your firm deal with them?

Some organizations respond on a case-by-case basis. This leaves room for inconsistency, since who is going to remember how a particular case was handled before, if it has been some time since it last occurred?

The firm's policy on as-of corrections may be constrained by its portfolio accounting system. Some permit such adjustments, while others don't. Or there may be a limit on how far back in time an adjustment can be made. If the firm wants greater flexibility, programming changes or a search for a new system might be in order. The systems side needs to be considered when this policy is discussed.

I'm unaware of any standard practices regarding as-of adjustments. Some firms simply don't allow them (i.e., if an error is discovered in a prior period, it isn't corrected). The obvious problem with this approach is that the firm is allowing erroneous information to be disseminated.

Other organizations establish *windows* of time when changes will be made; changes prior to this *window* will either not be permitted or will only be done if the magnitude of the adjustment exceeds some range.

This seems to be a reasonable approach. For example, the firm might establish a 3-month window. Any error that's discovered within this period will be corrected. Beyond that, the change must result in a certain basis point adjustment.

The ideal approach would be open-ended, where any change will be applied. The challenges here are several. One is that even minuscule changes will be applied. Some might argue whether this is really necessary.

If the client is receiving reports with changes to her returns, she may question the controls the organization has in place that permit the errors in the first place. This could be embarrassing to the firm.

The question should come down to the level of accuracy the firm wants to provide. If prior period errors will be tolerated, then changes won't be made. However, if the firm wants accurate reporting, then adjustments will be applied. Appropriate disclosures should accompany any reports with adjustments that explain the reason for the change. Hopefully, the client will appreciate the firm's desire to provide correct information, even if it reflects negatively on the firm.

Processing Composite-Level Adjustments

If the firm is in compliance with the AIMR Performance Presentation Standards, they will have the same issue to deal with when it comes to composite returns. Adjustments in account-level returns have a *ripple* effect that can result in adjustments to the account's composite(s).

Should adjustments be made to prior period reports? Here, the issue extends over to the marketing area, which often produces materials with composite returns on them. What if an error has occurred that affects the results being distributed to prospective clients?

Again, there is a variety of ways firms deal with these problems, from doing nothing, to addressing them on a case-by-case basis, to designating windows of time when adjustments will be made. The same points apply here as noted earlier.

I tend to favor the highest level of accuracy, but understand the attractiveness of the *window* approach. Applying no changes is generally unacceptable to me.

If the firm feels there are too many times when corrections must be made, then additional controls may be necessary to try to minimize their occurrence. The reality is, there will be the occasional adjustment. If they're too frequent, it may be an indication of inadequate controls or reporting being done prior to custodial reconciliation being completed.

Again, the firm's performance system may have constraints that limit adjustments. The policy should take these limits into consideration. If they're too constraining, the firm should consider system changes so that the desired level of flexibility is achieved.

MOVING ACCOUNTS IN/OUT OF COMPOSITES

AIMR permits some flexibility on the question of when accounts may be added to a composite. Originally, they called for this to happen at the beginning of the next reporting or measurement period.[1] They've since adjusted this, recognizing that firms need to get accounts established and that adding an account prematurely may cause problems if the account assets haven't been invested. This added flexibility exists but requires consistency.

Procedures should indicate how the account's composite(s) are determined. Perhaps a form will be used that will be signed off by the portfolio manager. A written procedure ensures consistency and understanding.

There are other times when accounts may have to be removed from a composite on a permanent or temporary basis. This may be due to a change in the account's investment objectives or some other event that causes it not to reasonably reflect the style or characteristics of the composite. AIMR requires that such movements be documented. The firm's policies and procedures should outline the situations when such movements may occur and how they are to be handled.

Definition of Discretion

AIMR provides a great deal of flexibility in determining discretion. It's up to each firm to decide how they will make this determination. Written policy statements can explain how the firm wants to handle the various scenarios that might arise, to avoid confusion and ensure consistency.

Nonmanaged Assets

Clients will often deposit securities with their manager with the instructions that these assets are not to be sold—the client simply wants all their securities in the same place to simplify record keeping. Should these assets be included in the performance calculation?

The answer is no, since the manager doesn't have full discretion over such assets. It's important that this point be clarified and that proper procedures exist to ensure these cases are handled correctly. The firm's system may not easily handle the segregation, but there are normally ways to work around these constraints.

CONTROLS

Controls should be established that cover access to the data. Pricing is an important area that needs to be controlled. Who has access to the prices? Who can change them? Since security prices have a direct impact on performance, it's important that such access be limited, preferably to individuals who don't have trading or money management responsibilities.

Certain security prices may not be available through electronic pricing sources. In these cases, the firm will often call various market makers to obtain prices. Again, a policy should be in place regarding how this is to be done, the number of market makers to be called, and which price to use in the event that more than one is received.

Constraints should also be provided on direct changes to account and composite level rates of return. Performance systems often permit these values to be overridden. Who has access to this functionality is something that should be controlled.

Imagine the problems a firm could be faced with if such controls didn't exist? If anyone could access this functionality? A portfolio manager or his assistant could alter the values to cast a better light on his performance. We know that such actions are possible, and the proper system controls can minimize the chances that they will occur.

Ideally, any change to either an account's or composite's return should be recorded in an audit trail for future reference. A report of changes or some other notification should be made to bring attention to the fact that such a change was made. The reason for the override should be recorded for future reference. The proper controls not only protect the firm but also communicate to all that they take these matters seriously.

CHAPTER SUMMARY

Investment firms require policies, procedures, and controls for many aspects of their business. Managing millions or billions of dollars of other people's money makes this a necessity. Since the reporting of performance has a major bearing on a firm's success—and often on the success and compensation of its employees—policies, procedures, and controls must be in place to ensure accuracy and completeness of reported returns.

The implementation of these procedures, etc., shouldn't be done as a formality. It's important that they're documented, communicated, understood, kept current, monitored, and enforced. Otherwise, the firm risks embarrassment at a minimum, and regulatory action or civil suits at the extreme.

ENDNOTES

1. Here, AIMR was a bit inconsistent. Some references called for the inclusion to occur at the beginning of the next *measurement* period, i.e., the period when composite returns are calculated, while at other times the materials referred to the next *reporting* period, i.e., the period when composite returns are reported. If these two periods are the same, then there wouldn't be a problem. However, if the firm reports composite returns *quarterly* based on *monthly* calculations, when should the new account be added to the composite? The author contacted an AIMR official regarding this and was told that as long as the firm added accounts in a *consistent* manner, it didn't matter which was done.

CHAPTER 12

The Future

Performance measurement isn't standing still. There's a continuing requirement to enhance the information that firms provide to their clients and prospects. Pressure is mounting to ensure that the information is highly accurate and meaningful.

Let's focus on the term "meaningful" for a moment. We've seen how the reporting of a rate-of-return figure, by itself, has little meaning. We need much more information to effectively evaluate the manager's performance and determine whether or not she has done a good job.

We need to be able to compare the return the manager achieved with some yardstick, be it a benchmark, index, peer group, or POD-generated value. We need to know what to attribute the manager's results to (e.g., good stock picking or currency changes that favored our portfolio). And we want to know what risk was taken in order to achieve the results. A rate-of-return value by itself has little meaning—we need more information to do a good job of evaluation.

As noted much earlier in this book, Peter Dietz and the Bank Administration Institute deserve a lot of credit for pointing out that the rates of return that were historically produced didn't properly measure the manager's performance because cash flows weren't taken into consideration. This lead to the introduction of *time-weighted rates of return,* and the refinement of the information hasn't stopped.

The increasing availability of accurate and timely performance results allows this information to become an integral part of the investment process. Managers don't have to *guess* how well they're doing. They'll have critical information available to help with their investment decisions.

AFTER-TAX RETURNS

One of the trends to ensure we're producing meaningful information is the desire for after-tax performance. This is, of course, only relevant to clients who pay taxes. But this is a fairly large portion of investors. Pretax performance is important, but many investors want to know what they are looking at *after* taxes are paid. This concept has been around a long time; however, as yet there are no standard approaches to calculating such a return.

One of the issues is what tax rate to use. Managers can't be expected to determine the tax rates for all of their clients. So, one approach is to use the highest possible rate, which will, of course, yield the lowest after-tax rate of return.

DAILY RATES OF RETURN

At one time, quarterly returns were considered adequate. Portfolios were revalued at the end of each quarter and a calculation performed. Later, there was a move to monthly returns.

In each case, cash flows were typically treated as if they occurred during the middle of the measurement period. In previous chapters, we saw the shortcomings of this approach.

We've known for some time that daily rates of return offer the greatest benefits:

- highest level of accuracy
- greater reporting capabilities, for both the firm and clients
- a high degree of flexibility for the calculation of odd-period rates of return
- allowance for prior period adjustments
- greater ease of calculation of subportfolio returns

GREATER EMPHASIS ON VERIFICATION OF
COMPLIANCE WITH STANDARDS

Regardless of what standards a firm is complying with, customers will want some assurance that their manager or prospective manager is, in fact, complying. It's difficult for a group like AIMR to require firms to undergo verification, due to the cost involved. However, over time, the marketplace will make this a much more common requirement, especially for firms vying for pension fund and other large institutional investor monies. Also, as the standards grow in complexity, firms will need some objective assurance that they are, in fact, complying.

STANDARD FOR RISK MEASUREMENT

Investors should always be conscious of the fact that any investment carries with it some level of risk. However, many managers fail to provide any indication of the underlying risk.

The SEC is considering imposing a requirement for disclosure of risk with mutual fund advertising. The challenge to date has been to come up with an acceptable measure. Over time, such a measure or measures will be defined.

For the private investor marketplace, a number of risk measures were discussed in chapter 6. Just as the industry now has performance presentation standards, we can expect to have risk measurement standards that will bring some level of uniformity to the reporting of risk, resulting in a more meaningful presentation of what a manager can do for his or her clients.

FLEXIBILITY IN REPORTING AND
ACCESS TO INFORMATION

Both managers and clients want to receive information in a variety of formats. The *slicing-and-dicing* of data, to provide information in the most meaningful fashion, is not unusual. Until recently, performance measurement reporting has been rather basic. This is no longer the case, as the investment function has grown to encompass a variety of security types, and international investing is becoming much more common.

With the volatility of the marketplace not slowing down, investors and portfolio managers want to be able to track their performance more closely. Regulatory and industry group disclosure requirements require increased flexibility, as does the need for firms to respond to a variety of requests for proposal for new business.

The firm's systems must be flexible enough to support these increasing requirements. On-demand reporting and access to data in a variety of formats will become a standard feature of any performance reporting system.

INTERNATIONAL FOCUS

The United States is much farther along than many other countries in performance measurement reporting. Initiatives have begun in a number of countries to establish consistent standards for performance reporting. Though these efforts are not nearly as far along as those of AIMR, they indicate that there is a recognition that a consistent method for presenting performance information is an attractive and necessary requirement.

One might ask why global standards are required? Perhaps it's an overused cliché, but the reality is that the world is becoming smaller and smaller. Advances in computer technology, telecommunications, and travel easily permit firms to compete for business across borders. Numerous U.S.-based money managers have established overseas offices, while many European firms have acquired U.S.-based firms or established offices in the States. Not only are money managers seeking investment opportunities beyond their own borders, they are looking for clients, too.

In order to establish a "level playing field" for this global competition, consistent presentation standards are required, just as they were for firms competing within the U.S.

While there is a need for uniformity, the effort to create it is resulting in the realization that there are many differences from one country to the next. For example, in some countries, it isn't unusual for the manager to also serve as the broker and custodian. Their fees are often bundled together. In the United States, this is usually not the case. Since fees typically come into play when firms are competing, a way is needed to clearly and fairly differentiate one firm from another.

Other differences are also coming into view. For example, some countries still don't mark-to-market their client portfolios; i.e., they don't price them to reflect appreciation or depreciation in the value of the holdings. Japan is one example. They are taking steps to require that client portfolios be priced on a regular basis.

Because some countries are not as far along in performance calculations, let alone presentations, global standards will incorporate both calculation and presentation guidelines.

The AIMR has been actively working with investment organizations from various countries to establish acceptable global standards. A few countries (e.g., Switzerland) have actually adopted the AIMR standards, which will help in coming to a common agreement. Hopefully, by the year 2000 we will have generally acceptable global standards for performance measurement and presentation.

INTERNET

Would any book be complete today without saying something about the Internet? The reality is that we should expect firms to be providing greater access to client information via the Internet, as confidence increases in the security of the information. The Internet provides a standardized platform for such access.

If there's a large shift in the market, clients will be able to access their account via the *Net*, to see what the impact on their investments was. The benefits are: improved customer satisfaction due to the availability of timely and accurate information, and a reduction in the number of phone inquiries that often occur when such shifts happen. We may also see the presence of performance information for prospective clients.

CHAPTER SUMMARY

Performance measurement is no longer an incidental task that's taken on by someone in the back office as a part-time effort. It's now a major function that requires attention and controls. The past few years suggest that the future will bring only greater emphasis to this area, with a requirement for more flexibility, accuracy, and consistency. There's also a growing need for expertise in perfor-

mance measurement and its related fields. The anticipated introduction of global presentation standards will bring about further
focus on a firm's calculations and presentations, necessitating continuing attention and control. There's no doubt that technology
will be available to provide the needed tools to support the continued expansion and interest in performance measurement.

Overview of the AIMR Performance Presentation Standards

The intention of AIMR Performance Presentation Standards (AIMR-PPS) is to provide a *level playing field* for providers of investment management services. By establishing a standard for the presentation of performance results, purchasers of such services will be able to compare apples to apples, rather than apples to oranges.

Historically, managers have reported results in various ways, making fair comparison difficult, if not impossible. Firms that comply with the AIMR-PPS will present performance results so as to make comparison much simpler.

Unlike previous performance standards, which focused on the actual rate-of-return calculation, the AIMR-PPS addresses the *presentation* of results, that is, how the results are shown to prospective clients.

PPS PUBLICATIONS

The AIMR-PPS began with the Financial Analysts Federation's efforts to standardize performance reporting. This effort started in 1986. Since then, a variety of materials have been published:

> *Performance Measurement: Setting The Standards, Interpreting the Numbers,* The Institute of Chartered Financial Analysts and the Financial Analysts Federation, 1989.

Report of the Performance Presentation Standards Implementation Committee, Association for Investment Management and Research, 1991.

Performance Reporting for Investment Managers: Applying the AIMR Performance Presentation Standards, Association for Investment Management and Research, 1991.

Answers to Common Questions about AIMR's Performance Presentation Standards, Association for Investment Management and Research, 1992.

Performance Presentation Standards 1993, Association for Investment Management and Research, 1993.

Second Edition AIMR Performance Presentation Standards Handbook 1997, Association for Investment Management and Research, 1996.

In addition, AIMR has published answers to questions in a variety of formats. The "official" AIMR Standards is the *Second Edition AIMR Performance Presentation Standards Handbook 1997,* which was published at the end of 1996. Shortly after it was published, the SEC issued a no-action letter (see Appendix C) that alters some of the information contained in this book. I suspect that we will see another revision printed in a shorter time frame than between the first and second issues.

EFFECTIVE DATE OF COMPLIANCE

The AIMR-PPS standards went into effect January 1, 1993. AIMR established subsequent dates for compliance for certain types of accounts (e.g., January 1, 1994, for taxable and international, other than Canada; July 1, 1995, for wrap-fee accounts). For a variety of reasons, some firms did not comply immediately with the standards. Perhaps they were waiting to see what other firms did, or the cost and time required may have been excessive.

Since AIMR states that retroactive compliance is an option, one might interpret this to mean that if you come into compliance effective January 1, 1997, going back to 1993 would constitute retroactive compliance, and would therefore be an option. This is not the case.

As we discussed at length in chapter 9, to comply with the AIMR-PPS, a firm must be in compliance as of January 1, 1993 (for nontaxable accounts; later for other account types), or as of inception date, if the inception of the firm is after January 1, 1993. In general, if a firm does not go back to the earlier date, they must wait *ten* years before they can state that they meet the standards; that is, if a firm becomes compliant effective January 1, 1997, but was in existence in 1993 and chooses not to comply to the earlier date, they must wait until January 1, 2007, before they can state they're in compliance with the AIMR-PPS.

AIMR provides some exceptions to this. For example, if a firm is unable to comply because of loss of records, an exception can be made (again, as discussed in chapter 9). However, a firm that falls into this category should consult with AIMR for clarification.

COMPOSITES—THE BASIS FOR THE STANDARDS

A composite is a collection of portfolios (or portions of portfolios) that have similar investment styles and objectives. Firms can have from one to many composites, and portfolios may be included in one or more. Maintenance of composites (creating, adding, and removing accounts) is a task that requires a great deal of attention.

COMPOSITE RATE OF RETURN

AIMR requires composite returns to be asset-weighted (see chapter 9). Equal-weighted returns are encouraged. The author strongly recommends that both be available to respond to various needs from prospective clients.

DISCLOSURE DOCUMENTS

The AIMR-PPS has to do with the *presentation* of performance results. Therefore, certain disclosures are required:

- ten-year history of returns (or since inception, if the firm has been in existence less than ten years)
- annual rates of return

- a measure of dispersion (e.g., standard deviation, high-low, asset-weighted standard deviation)
- the availability of a list and description of the firm's other composites
- the number of portfolios that are contained in the composite
- the amount of assets in the composite
- the percentage of assets in the composite relative to the firm's total assets under management
- an indication if segments of balanced portfolios are included (if they are, the method used for allocating cash must also be indicated [see chapter 3])
- whether returns have been calculated gross-of-fees or net-of-fees
- the firm's fee schedule
- if the returns are net-of-fees, the average weighted management fee must be disclosed
- if returns were calculated based on settlement date, this must be disclosed; no disclosure is necessary if trade date was used
- if any non-fee-paying accounts are included
- the use and extent of leverage
- if there has been a material change in the personnel responsible for investment management
- the effective date of compliance

As noted above, AIMR requires a 10 years of results (or less if the firm hasn't been in existence for 10 years). If there are any periods for which results aren't in compliance, then this must be disclosed and the reason why the period isn't in compliance must be stated.

DEFINITION OF "FIRM"

The first version of the AIMR-PPS [AIMR 1993] had rather stringent requirements for firm definition. Problems arose because many banks and insurance companies wanted to comply, but found it extremely challenging because of the work that would be involved. For example, a bank that essentially had two lines of business—

trust accounts and institutional—would have had to bring both into compliance in order to satisfy AIMR's requirements.

The newer version of the standards [AIMR 1996] has broadened the definition considerably. It now permits affiliates, subsidiaries, and even nonlegal elements of an organization to claim compliance, as long as it holds itself out as being separate from the other parts of the business. This expanded flexibility should make compliance much easier for numerous firms.

Clover Capital Management, Inc., No-Action Letter

The SEC issues no-action letters to indicate that they will not recommend enforcement action under certain conditions. One of the
most commonly cited letters is the 1986 Clover Capital Management letter. Both the no-action letter and the Clover letter that re-
quested it are shown below.

1986 SEC No-Act. LEXIS 2883

Investment Advisers Act of 1940 – Rule 106(4)-1(a)(5)

Oct. 28, 1986

Clover Capital Management, Inc.

TOTAL NUMBER OF LETTERS: 2

SEC-REPLY-1: SECURITIES AND EXCHANGE COMMISSION
WASHINGTON, D.C. 20549
OCT 28 1986
RESPONSE OF THE OFFICE OF CHIEF COUNSEL
DIVISION OF INVESTMENT MANAGEMENT
Our Ref. No. 86-264-CC
Clover Capital Management, Inc.
File No. 801-27041

Your letter of June 3, 1986, requests our assurance that we would not recommend any enforcement action to the Commission under Rule 206(4)-1(a)(5) of the Investment Advisers Act of 1940 ("Act") if Clover Capital Management, Inc. ("Clover"), a registered investment adviser, uses investment results derived from a "model" portfolio in advertisements (hereinafter "model results"). As described more fully in your letter, the model portfolio was established by Clover on January 1, 1985, and consists of the same securities that Clover recommended to clients during the time period. As your letter notes, Clover's investment approach incorporates the philosophy that all of its clients should invest in the same securities, with variances in specific client objectives being addressed via the asset allocation process (i.e., the relative weighting of stocks, bonds, and cash equivalents in each account). Thus, while the model results do not correspond directly to the results achieved by any actual client account, Clover has managed the model portfolio with the same investment philosophy it uses for client accounts. Because of the significant degree of interest in this issue, and in the related issue of advisers using actual investment results of client accounts under management in advertisements (hereinafter "actual results"), we wish to take this opportunity to set forth the staff's view on these issues.

Section 206 of the Act prohibits certain transactions by any investment adviser, whether registered or exempt from registration pursuant to Section 203(b) of the Act. Under paragraph (4) of Section 206, the Commission has authority to adopt rules defining acts, practices, and courses of business that are fraudulent, deceptive, or manipulative. Pursuant to this authority, the Commission adopted Rule 206(4)-1, which defines the use of certain specific types of advertisements[1] by advisers as fraudulent, deceptive, or manipulative.[2] Although the rule does not specifically prohibit an adviser from using model or actual results, or prescribe the manner of advertising these results, paragraph (5) of the rule makes it a fraudulent, deceptive, or manipulative act for any investment adviser to distribute, directly or indirectly, any advertisement that contains any untrue statement of a material fact or is otherwise false or misleading.[3] Accordingly, the applicable legal standard governing the advertising of model or actual results is that contained in paragraph (5) of the rule, i.e., whether the particular advertisement is false or misleading.[4]

The staff no longer takes the position, as it did a number of years ago, that the use of model or actual results in an advertisement is per se fraudulent under Section 206(4) and the rules thereunder, particularly Rule 206(4)-1(a)(5).[5] Rather, this determination is one of fact, and we believe the use of model or actual results in an advertisement would be false or misleading under Rule 206(4)-1(a)(5) if it implies, or a reader would infer from it, something about the adviser's competence or about future investment results that would not be true had the advertisement included all material facts.[6] Any adviser using such an advertisement must ensure that the advertisement discloses all material facts concerning the model or actual results so as to avoid these unwarranted implications or inferences.[7] Because of the factual nature of the determination, the staff, as a matter of policy, does not review any specific advertisements.[8] Therefore, we express no opinion regarding your proposed advertisements.

In order to assist advisers who advertise model or actual results, we wish to take this opportunity to set forth certain advertising practices the staff believes are inappropriate under Rule 206(4)-1(a)(5). The list is not intended to address all advertising practices prohibited by Rule 206(4)-1(a)(5) and does not create a "safe harbor" that may be relied upon by an adviser as an exclusive list of the factors that must be considered in determining the type of disclosure necessary when advertising model or actual results. Items (1)–(6) below apply to both model and actual results; Items (7)–(10) apply to model results; and Item (11) applies to actual results.

In the staff's view, Rule 206(4)-1(a)(5) prohibits an advertisement that:

Model and Actual Results

(1) Fails to disclose the effect of material market or economic conditions on the results portrayed (e.g., an advertisement stating that the accounts of the adviser's clients appreciated in value 25% without disclosing that the market generally appreciated 40% during the same period);[9]

(2) Includes model or actual results that do not reflect the deduction of advisory fees, brokerage or other commissions, and any other expenses that a client would have paid or actually paid;

(3) Fails to disclose whether and to what extent the results portrayed reflect the reinvestment of dividends and other earnings;

(4) Suggests or makes claims about the potential for profit without also disclosing the possibility of loss;[10]

(5) Compares model or actual results to an index without disclosing all material facts relevant to the comparison (e.g., an advertisement that compares model results to an index without disclosing that the volatility of the index is materially different from that of the model portfolio);[11]

(6) Fails to disclose any material conditions, objectives, or investment strategies used to obtain results portrayed (e.g., the model portfolio contains equity stocks that are managed with a view towards capital appreciation);

(7) Fails to disclose prominently the limitations inherent in results,[12] particularly the fact that such results do not represent actual trading and that they may not reflect the impact that material economic and market factors might have had on the adviser's decision-making if the adviser were actually managing clients' money;

(8) Fails to disclose, if applicable, that the conditions, objectives, or investment strategies of the model portfolio changed materially during the time period portrayed in the advertisement and, if so, the effect of such change on the results portrayed;

(9) Fails to disclose, if applicable, that any of the securities in, or the investment strategies followed with respect to, the model portfolio do not relate, or only partially relate, to the type of advisory services currently offered by the adviser (e.g., the model includes some types of securities that the adviser no longer recommends for its clients);[13]

(10) Fails to disclose, if applicable, that the adviser's clients had investment results materially different from the results portrayed in the model;

Actual Results

(11) Fails to disclose prominently, if applicable, that the results portrayed relate only to a select group of the adviser's clients, the basis on which the selection was made, and the effect of this practice on the results portrayed, if material.[14]

As we agreed, this response will be made public immediately.

Thomas P. Lemke
Chief Counsel

INQUIRY-1
Clover Capital Management, Inc.
5 Tobey Village Office Park
Pittsford, New York 14531
(716) 385-6000

June 3, 1986

Mr. Thomas P. Lemke
Chief Counsel
Division of Investment Management
Securities & Exchange Commission
450 5th Street N.W.
Washington, D.C. 20549

Dear Mr. Lemke:

Clover Capital Management, Inc., is an investment counseling firm registered with the S.E.C. under the Investment Advisers Act of 1940. I have enclosed a copy of a letter we recently received from Mr. Frank Morrison of the S.E.C.'s New York City office informing us that our use of a Model Portfolio for tracking the firm's investment record violates Rule 206(4)-1(a)(5). In a subsequent telephone conversation with Mr. Dolan, an associate of Mr. Morrison's, we were made aware that your office has the authority to rule on such matters on a case-by-case basis and to issue "No Action Letters", where warranted. Please consider our case based on the following information:

1. Clover Capital Management, Inc. is an investment management firm founded in October, 1984 by Michael E. Jones, CFA and Geoffrey Rosenberger, CFA. We had several very successful years experience as investment analysts and portfolio managers at the firm of Manning and Napier Advisors, Inc. In starting our new firm, we were faced with the dilemma of providing prospective clients with an understanding of our prior and current investment results and style of management. In dealing with this problem, we aspired to maintain the highest possible ethical standards. Thus, we have not represented our previous firm's record as our own or as an indica-

tion of Clover Capital Management's ability. We have chosen to forego discussion of our specific results on clients prior to forming Clover Capital.

However, as you know, the issue of demonstrating the firm's competence and style of management is important in presenting our service to prospective clients. Our problem is to find a way to show what we are doing in our research and management effort at Clover Capital Management, Inc. without violating client confidentiality and without misrepresenting our performance to the public.

One approach to this problem involves presenting the performance achieved among our account base. However, the securities markets have been quite volatile in the past 18 months and our client base has grown consistently each month. As a result, a portfolio that started January, 1985 has different results than one we began in September, 1985. To take an arithmetic average of each client's actual results and present that as the firm's track record would be misleading due to the significant standard deviation from client to client based on date of entry to our firm's management.

On the other hand, to just pick one or two client portfolios would be equally misleading because of differences in the timing of cash flows, specific client objectives and other considerations which may be unique to a small sample of accounts. We recognized at the outset that this would be the case. We also recognized this presentation of results would not satisfy questions on portfolio construction and investment style with respect to diversification, portfolio beta, asset allocation and related items. The raw results would also be impossible to verify without violating client confidentiality.

The most accurate, verifiable reflection of our true investment product, in light of these circumstances, was to establish a Model Portfolio as of January 1, 1985, which we would manage exactly as we would a tax-exempt client portfolio with no restrictions as to income and without any cash flow into or out of the fund.

2. The securities purchased and sold in the Model Portfolio are also purchased and sold in our client accounts under management at the time of the transaction. It is important to note that our investment approach incorporates the philosophy that all of our clients should own the same stock selections, with variances in specific client objectives being addressed via the asset allocation process (the relative weightings) of stocks, bonds, and cash equivalents in each account. For example, when we make a decision to invest in a common stock, we also decide what percentage of each client's assets we wish to commit to that particular equity. Differences in client objectives are reflected in the weightings placed for each account. Most of our accounts are tax exempt retirement funds with conservative objectives and therefore receive similar weightings. However some clients have differing objectives due to current income requirements, moral considerations, "equities only" restrictions, and other factors which may alter the weightings in specific investments. The Model Portfolio weightings are determined according to it's [sic] stated hypothetical structure as a conservative pension fund.

3. We have taken extensive steps to insure that the reporting format is an objective one. The independent accounting firm of Davie, Kaplan & Braverman was hired to audit our efforts in this effort. To place a purchase or sale transaction, we call Davie, Kaplan & Braverman prior to the 9:30 a.m. market opening. All transactions are assumed to occur at the prior day's closing price as listed in *The Wall Street Journal*, which Davie Kaplan & Braverman can easily verify. Commissions are charged against each transaction based on a 35% discount from the Cowen & Co. commission schedule, which is roughly the same commission expense level we incur in our client accounts. Investment management fees are also charged against the portfolio in line with our standard client fee schedule.

4. In addition to monitoring the purchase and sale transactions in the Model Portfolio, Davie, Kaplan & Braverman also accounts for the dividend and interest income, commission charges and investment management fee reimbursement in the portfolio. The quarterly investment performance reports are also compiled and issued by Davie Kaplan & Braverman, not by Clover Capital Manage-

ment, Inc. There is a measure of independence and objectivity to our Model Portfolio Report and its calculations which may be lacking in the investment performance figures reported by other investment management firms.

5. We feel it is important that the prospective clients see how the investment returns being presented to them were achieved. Use of the Model Portfolio allows people to see what stocks we hold and what the recent transaction activity in the account has been. They can develop a feel for our investment style that would otherwise be difficult to achieve prior to entering into a relationship with our firm.

6. The only reference the report makes to investment results is on an absolute return basis. The report only records a percentage increase in asset value. It makes no comparisons to any stock or bond market indexes.

We believe that, for the above reasons, our Model Portfolio report provides an excellent proxy for our investment approach and track record. However, we also understand the Commission's concern about the potential for misunderstanding of the Model's purpose on the part of the public. Therefore, we are willing to incorporate the following statement (or a similar version) into our report:

"The Clover Capital Management, Inc. Model Portfolio represents a fictional account which Clover Capital Management, Inc. ("CCM") attempts to manage in a manner similar to that of a tax-exempt client fund with no need for special portfolio considerations. The investment objective for this portfolio over a four year period is to exceed, by at least 3%, the compound annual rate of return on a Treasury note with a four year maturity and at the same time to limit volatility in such a way as to avoid the incurrance [sic] of a negative return during any calendar year.

It is CCM's intention to own the same securities in each client portfolio with similar objectives. Securities transactions will not be undertaken in the Model Portfolio until at least half the existing accounts under management have completed the contemplated transaction. However, circumstances such as market fluctuations may exist which may prevent an individual CCM client from owning one or more of the specific securities held in the Model Portfolio.

Since the account is fictional, there can be no assurance that a CCM client would have achieved similar rates of return over the same time frame. In addition, since the time period in question is a historical one, there can be no assurance that future results achieved by the firm's clients will in any way resemble those represented by the Model Portfolio."

We believe that use of the Model Portfolio is the most valid approximation we can provide a prospective client as to what our investment activity has been since January 1, 1985. While no form of investment performance measurement is entirely without fault, of all those available to us this approach is the one which provides the least amount of bias. We therefore respectfully request that you confirm that you will not recommend enforcement action if we continue to use the Model Portfolio in the manner stated in this letter and with the explanatory and disclaimer language found in the enclosed Model Portfolio copy.

Your assistance in this matter is most appreciated.

Sincerely,

Clover Capital Management, Inc.
By Geoffrey Rosenberger, President

ENDNOTES

1. Rule 206(4)-1(b) generally defines an "advertisement" to include any communication addressed to more than one person that offers any investment advisory service with regard to securities.

2. For example, Rule 206(4)-1 prohibits an adviser from using advertisements that include testimonials (paragraph (a)) or that refer to past specific recommendations unless certain information is provided (paragraph (b)). The staff is currently reviewing Rule 206(4)-1 to determine whether it needs to be revised or updated. See Investment Advisers Act Rel. No. 1033 (Aug. 6, 1986).

3. As a general matter, whether any advertisement is false or misleading will depend on the particular facts and circumstances surrounding its use, including (1) the form as well as the content of the advertisement, (2) the implications or inferences arising out of the advertisement in its total context, and (3) the sophistication of the prospective client. See, e.g., Covato/Lipsitz, Inc. (pub. avail. Oct 23, 1981) ("Covato"); Edward F. O'Keefe (pub. avail. Apr. 13, 1978) ("O'Keefe"); Anametrics Investment Management (pub. avail. May 5, 1977) ("Anametrics").

4. Of course, if an advertisement containing model or actual results also includes any of the specific advertising practices addressed by paragraphs (a)(1)-(a)(4) of the Rule 206(4)-1, the advertisement would have to comply with the requirements of these paragraphs.

5. See, e.g., A.R. Schmeidler & Co. (pub. avail. June 1, 1976); Schield Stock Services, Inc. (pub. avail. Feb. 26, 1972).

6. See, e.g., Anametrics, Covato, and O'Keefe, supra noted 3.

7. Id.

8. See, e.g., Anametrics, supra note 3.

9. Id.

10. See F. Eberstadt & Co., Inc. (pub. avail. July 2, 1978).

11. See, e.g.,, Anametrics, supra note 3; Multinational Investments, Inc. (pub. avail. Sept. 17, 1977).

12. With respect to model results, the staff recognizes that advisers may wish to advertise model results derived from model portfolios that differ in form and structure from that presented by your letter. We believe that to the extent it is more difficult to verify or objectively test the criteria underlying the model portfolio in question, the disclosure obligation of the adviser would correspondingly increase.

13. See, e.g., Covato, supra note 3.

14. See, e.g., O'Keefe, supra note 3.

AIMR No-Action Letter

On December 18, 1996, the SEC issued a no-action letter that addressed several important aspects of performance reporting. This letter was in response to the Association for Investment Management & Research's request for relief from SEC enforcement. The text of both the SEC no-action letter and AIMR's letter follow.

AIMR's letter is dated December 3, 1996, a mere two weeks before the SEC's letter. The reader should *not* interpret this to mean that it took AIMR only two weeks to get a response from the SEC. This effort took 15 months of negotiations and dialogue. The SEC insisted that AIMR file new letters, not amendments, as this effort progressed.

December 18, 1996   Ref No. 96-21-CC, File No. 132-3

Association for Investment Management and Research

Response of the Office of Chief Counsel, Division of Investment Management

Your letter of December 3, 1996 requests our assurance that we would not recommend enforcement action to the Commission if, in presenting performance information, an investment adviser ("Presenting Adviser") that seeks to comply with certain minimum performance presentation standards ("PPS") developed by the Association for Investment Management and Research ("AIMR") advertises performance as follows:[1]

(1) The Presenting Adviser provides gross and net-of-fee performance for composites of the Presenting Adviser's accounts that include mutual fund accounts, provided that the gross and net performance are both presented with equal prominence in a format designed to facilitate ease of comparison and are accompanied by appropriate disclosure explaining how the performance figures were calculated and not identifying any specific mutual fund included within the composite.

(2) The Presenting Adviser includes the performance of both its non-wrap fee accounts and wrap fee accounts in the same composite, and calculates the composite performance by deducting from the performance of non-wrap fee accounts a "model fee" equal to the highest fee charged to a wrap fee account in the composite.

(3) The Presenting Adviser calculates net-of-fee performance for an account managed by a number of advisers including the Presenting Adviser ("multi-manager accounts"), by deducting from the performance of that portion of the account managed by the Presenting Adviser those fees related to the management of that portion by the Presenting Adviser, such as transaction costs and all fees paid to the Presenting Adviser or any of its affiliates.

The Presentation of Composites Including Mutual Fund and Non-Mutual Fund Accounts

You first inquire whether a Presenting Adviser may provide, in advertisements and one-on-one presentations, both gross- and net-of-fee performance results for composites[2] that include both mutual funds and non-mutual fund accounts. Specifically, you represent that a Presenting Adviser would display both gross and net performance results with equal prominence and in a format designed to facilitate ease of comparison of the gross and net results. You also represent that these results would be accompanied by disclosure explaining how the performance figures were calculated.[3] Finally, to avoid any inference that the presentation is a promotion or advertisement for a particular mutual fund, you state that this disclosure will not identify any specific mutual fund included within the composite.

Section 206(4) of the Investment Advisers Act of 1940 ("Advisers Act") prohibits any act, practice or course of business that the Commission, by rule, defines as fraudulent, deceptive or manipulative. Rule 206(4)-1(a)(5) under the Advisers Act provides that it is a fraudulent, deceptive or manipulative act for any investment adviser to distribute, directly or indirectly, any advertisement that contains any untrue statement of a material fact or that is otherwise false or misleading. In Clover Capital Management, Inc. (pub. avail. Oct 28, 1986) ("*Clover Capital*"), the staff interpreted Rule 206(4)-1(a)(5) to prohibit advertisements that include performance results that do not reflect the deduction of advisory fees, brokerage commissions, and any other expenses that a client would have paid or actually paid.[4]

The first issue presented by your letter is whether an investment adviser may distribute an advertisement that presents both gross- and net-of-fee performance information for a composite of the adviser's accounts. You maintain that an adviser would not violate Rule 206(4)-1(a)(5) if it distributes an advertisement presenting gross and net performance with equal prominence and in a format designed to facilitate ease of comparison, provided that the advertisement contains sufficient disclosure to ensure that the material presented is not misleading. The staff agrees that such an advertisement would not be prohibited by the Rule.[5]

The second issue raised by your letter is whether the presentation of a gross-of-fee composite that includes the performance of one or more mutual funds managed by the adviser would be subject to the requirements governing investment company advertisements and sales literature. Under the Securities Act of 1933 (Rule 482(e) (3)) and the Investment Company Act (Rule 34b-1),[6] any performance information in mutual fund advertisements or sales literature must include standardized total return calculated under a formula that requires the deduction of all fees and expenses paid by the fund. You represent, however, that the disclosure accompanying the composite would not identify any specific mutual fund that is included in the composite. In our view, as long as an advertisement for investment advisory services does not include an explicit or implicit reference to a particular fund, it would not be an advertisement for a fund.[7] Therefore, in our view the standardized performance requirements of Rule 482 and Rule 34b-1 referenced above would not apply to such an advertisement.

The Presentation of Performance of a Composite Including Wrap Fee and Non-Wrap Fee Accounts

You propose that Presenting Advisers deduct from non-wrap fee accounts that are included with wrap fee accounts in a composite, a "model fee" equal to the highest fee charged to a wrap fee account in the composite. You represent that the highest fee charged to a wrap fee account would be higher than any fee charged to a non-wrap fee account included in the composite.[8]

In such a case, the staff would not consider it a fraudulent or deceptive practice under Rule 206(4)-1 if an adviser presents net performance that reflects the deduction of actual fees from wrap fee accounts and the deduction of a model fee, equal to the highest fee charged to a wrap fee account, from non-wrap fee accounts, provided that the advertisement contains sufficient disclosure to ensure that the information presented is not misleading.[9]

The Calculation of Net Performance Results

You request our views regarding which fees a Presenting Adviser must deduct in calculating the net-of-fee performance of a "multi-manager" account.[10] You propose that, for purposes of calculating the net-of-fee performance of an adviser's portion of a multi-manager account included in a composite, a Presenting Adviser should be required to deduct only those fees related to its management of the account. You represent that performance results would be accompanied by disclosure that specifically identifies the types of fees deducted.

In *Clover Capital*, the staff took the position that performance information in an advertisement should reflect the deduction of "advisory fees, brokerage or other commissions, and any other expense that a client would have paid or actually paid." In Investment Company Institute (pub. avail. July 24, 1987), the staff took the position that custodial fees need not be deducted from net performance, and stated that "information about the fees the adviser charged clients in the sample is material to evaluating the investment experience of those clients and the adviser's competence."

In the staff's view the fees relevant to an evaluation of the investment experience of the adviser's clients and of the adviser's competence are those fees or charges related to the adviser's management of the account. The staff believes that, at a minimum, these fees and charges include: 1) all transaction costs; and 2) all fees or charges paid to the adviser or an affiliate of the adviser.

Our position with respect to the calculation of net performance is not limited to the performance of multi-manager accounts. The net-of-fee performance of any investment advisory account may be calculated by deducting only the fees described above.

Conclusion

We would not recommend enforcement action to the Commission if an adviser includes performance information in advertisements and one-one-one presentations calculated and set forth in the manner described above. This position is based on the facts and representations set forth in your letter and described above. You should note that any different facts or representations might require a different conclusion.

/s/

Eileen M. Smiley
Senior Counsel

December 3, 1996

Jack W. Murphy, Esquire
Chief Counsel
Division of Investment Management
Securities and Exchange Commission
450 Fifth Street, N.W.
Washington, D.C. 20549

Dear Mr. Murphy:

The Association for Investment Management and Research
(AIMR)[11] is writing seeking no-action assurances from the Staff of
the Securities and Exchange Commission (SEC) with regard to certain investment advisory management firm's (investment adviser)
performance issues related to the AIMR Performance Presentation
Standards (AIMR-PPS) currently being considered by AIMR's PPS
Implementation Committee.

SUMMARY

AIMR requests no-action relief from the SEC Staff with regard to
the following proposed clarifications to the AIMR PPS standards:

(1) Non-wrap fee accounts, which are included in the same
composite as wrap fee accounts and are to be presented to wrap fee
customers, must reflect a "model-wrap fee" equal to the highest fee
charged against the wrap fee accounts in the composite when the
model-wrap fee is higher than the actual non-wrap investment
management fee.

(2) Composites that include mutual fund assets must be presented net of fees, and may be presented on a gross of fee basis. The
gross and net of fee results must be presented with equal prominence in a format designed to facilitate ease of comparison. Disclosure must not identify any specific mutual fund the performance of
which is included in the composites.

(3) Net of fee presentations for composites that include an investment adviser's performance managing a portion of the assets
of a multi-managed account may reflect the deduction of only
those fees related to the management of the assets by the adviser. A
statement of those fees and costs that have been deducted must be
included with the performance.

BACKGROUND

An essential element of AIMR's mission is the establishment of the highest ethical standards required to be followed by all AIMR members and candidates for the CFA designation program (members). To assist its members in complying with these ethical standards, AIMR and its predecessor organization, the Financial Analysts Federation, developed and adopted the AIMR-PPS standards. The AIMR-PPS standards identify minimum levels of accepted ethical standards for presenting investment performance.[12] They are intended to promote fair representation and full disclosure in presentations of investment performance results. The AIMR-PPS standards also promote uniformity and comparability results of various investment advisers. The AIMR-PPS standards satisfy several additional goals; they improve the service offered to investment adviser clients, enhance the professionalism of the industry, and bolster self-regulation.

Since 1990, the AIMR-PPS Implementation Committee, a standing AIMR committee, is responsible for the ongoing implementation and interpretation of the AIMR-PPS standards. As warranted, and with AIMR Board approval, the Implementation Committee provides clarification and modification of the AIMR-PPS standards.

A basic element of the AIMR-PPS standards is the use of composites in investment performance presentations. A composite is the aggregation of portfolios or asset classes, which are managed with a similar strategy or investment objective, into a single performance presentation.[13] In a composite format, prospective clients are shown the performance results of the investment adviser firm without displaying individual account performance. Prospective clients are advised that a list and description of all of an investment adviser firm's composites are available upon request. Information regarding any specific account is not provided in the composite presentation.

The AIMR-PPS standards require the use of composites because they help to ensure that investors receive a fair and complete representation of an adviser's past performance record. Composites ensure that *all* accounts sharing a particular investment style, strategy and objective are included in performance presentations, thus providing a more complete record than the use of a "representative account" or partial composite that leaves out accounts that have terminated.

The Implementation Committee has received numerous inquiries concerning the AIMR-PPS standards as they relate to the presentation of investment results under certain circumstances. AIMR often assists its members in complying with SEC requirements in furtherance of high ethical standards in the investment management industry. In this connection, over the last few months the following issues have arisen for which further clarification from the Staff is needed:

(1) Whether non-wrap fee accounts included in the same composite as wrap fee accounts, to be presented to wrap fee customers, can reflect a "model-wrap fee" equal to the highest fee charged against the wrap fee accounts in the composite when the "model-wrap fee" is higher than the actual non-wrap investment management fee.

(2) Whether a composite including mutual funds can be presented to potential clients on a gross of fee basis if it is also presented on a net of fee basis, and gross and net of fee results are presented with equal prominence in a format designed to facilitate ease of comparison and no specific mutual fund included in the composite is identified.

(3) Whether a composite that includes investment adviser accounts that consist of a portion of the assets of a multi-managed account can be presented to potential clients on a net of fee basis after deducting only those fees and costs related to the management of the assets by the adviser, including transaction costs and all fees and charges paid by the account to the investment adviser or an affiliate of the investment adviser, provided that it is accompanied with a statement indicating those fees and costs that have been deducted.

WRAP FEE ACCOUNTS

Unlike traditional separate investment accounts, in which customers are charged separate fees for the services they receive, a single fee is charged against a wrap fee account for several combined services. As a result, management fees, transaction costs and other service costs in a wrap fee account are difficult to separate and identify.

AIMR recommends that wrap fee accounts be grouped in separate composites from non-wrap fee accounts. The performance of wrap fee composites must be shown on a net of fee basis. This requirement comes, in part, from the belief that wrap fee customers should be shown a composite which accurately illustrates the fee and the performance of relevant wrap fee accounts. This inclusion of low-fee paying non-wrap fee accounts into the composite could improperly distort the results and mislead customers.

The use of separate wrap fee and non-wrap fee composites, however, may not always provide wrap fee customers with a complete picture of the investment adviser's performance history. For example, the inclusion of non-wrap fee accounts in wrap fee account composites may be the only method of presenting a meaningful performance history to wrap fee customers for investment management firms with few wrap fee accounts, or a limited history of participating in a wrap fee program. In addition, because transaction costs in wrap fee accounts generally are inseparable from management fees, the presentation of wrap fee composites on a gross of fee basis reflects the deduction of no transaction or other fees. Therefore, a combination of wrap fee and non-wrap fee accounts in one composite must always be shown on a net of fee basis. To provide guidance in this situation, the Implementation Committee[14] has determined to recommend, subject to Staff concurrence, that investment management firms who combine wrap fee and non-wrap fee accounts in the same composite, for purposes of selling wrap fee accounts, deduct from the non-wrap fee accounts a "model-wrap fee" equal to the highest fee charged against the wrap fee accounts in the composite when the "model-wrap fee" is higher than the actual investment management fee deducted from the non-wrap fee accounts.[15] A copy of the fee schedule would be presented with the composite as required by the AIMR-PPS standards. To use this mixed model fee approach, however, the highest fee charged to any wrap fee account will be higher than any fee charged to a non-wrap fee account included in the composite. These requirements protect against misrepresentation of performance or fees and minimize investor confusion.

The AIMR-PPS standards provide guidance as to appropriate method for the deduction of the "model fee." It is the same procedure applicable to the deduction of management fees when management fees are paid outside of the investment account. This same provision is to be used by the investment adviser when applying the highest fee charged against the wrap fee accounts in the composite to the non-wrap fee accounts included in the same wrap fee composite. The fee is to be allocated over the measurement period at least quarterly. The fee treatment must be applied consistently over all portfolios, composites and time periods.

The SEC Staff has previously permitted the use of model fees when advertising historical performance in *Securities Industry Association* (November 27, 1989) (SIA). In SIA, the Staff permitted the use of model fees for advisers that could not reconstruct actual fees for purposes of advertising historical net performance.[16] Although the Staff in SIA permitted model fees to be used only during a temporary time period, the Staff's position reflects a recognition that model fees may be appropriate in limited circumstances. More recently in *J. P. Morgan Investment Management, Inc. (May 7, 1996)* the SEC staff permitted the use of performance advertising that reflects the deduction of a model fee provided the resulting performance figures would be no higher than those that would have resulted from the deduction of the actual fees.

The SEC Staff has indicated a willingness to consider the use of model fees in the circumstances described above. Therefore, we request confirmation that the Staff will not recommend enforcement action against AIMR members and others that claim compliance with the AIMR-PPS standards for following the AIMR-PPS Implementation Committee's interpretation and using model fees in presenting non-wrap fee and wrap fee accounts in the same composite.

COMPOSITE FORMAT

The AIMR-PPS standards currently recommend that investment management firms present their composite performance (to non-wrap fee customers) on a gross of fee basis unless to do so would conflict with applicable law.

The AIMR-PPS Implementation Committee takes the position, subject to Staff concurrence, that investment advisers who act as advisers to separate investment accounts as well as mutual funds[17] may include mutual fund accounts in a composite on a gross of fee basis, and must also present composite results on a net of fee basis, if the requirements of the AIMR-PPS standards are followed. In addition, the gross and net of fee composite results must be presented with equal prominence in a format designed to facilitate ease of comparison. The accompanying disclosure must not identify any specific mutual fund included in the composite.

In *Investment Company Institute* (August 24, 1997) (ICI1), the Staff stated that "the primary purpose of advertising actual results derived from a sample of client accounts is to show prospective clients the kind of investment experience they might have had as clients of that adviser and to permit them to evaluate the adviser's competence and ability to manage accounts." The Staff further expressed the concern that advertising actual results of advisory accounts on a gross of fee basis may imply, or may lead a customer to infer, something about the investment experience that would not be true if the advertisement included information about actual fees and expenses.[18] The Staff later permitted in *Investment Company Institute* (September 23, 1988) (ICI2) the use of performance data on a gross of fee basis in one-on-one presentations where the client has the opportunity to discuss with the adviser the types of fees that the client will pay.[19]

In one-on-one presentations aimed at separate investment account clients and not mutual fund sales, the investment experience relevant to customer accounts would not include fees imposed in a mutual fund context. Moreover, any mutual fund's performance would appear in a composite in coordination with other investment results. The accompanying disclosure would not identify any specific mutual fund included within the composite. In the absence of performance related to a specific mutual fund, customers would be unable to draw any inference about any particular mutual fund's performance. The inclusion of the mutual fund's performance would be solely illustrative of the investment adviser's performance in managing assets with similar objectives, risk factors, and other common features that are appropriately included in a composite. Both gross and net of fee composite results are required to be presented with equal prominence in a format designed to facilitate ease of comparison.

AIMR believes that the presentation of mutual fund performance included in composite investment results on a gross of fee basis as described above is the most relevant and appropriate method of describing an investment adviser's performance history. As such, AIMR requests the Staff's assurance that it will not recommend enforcement action against AIMR members and others that claim compliance with the AIMR-PPS standards for including mutual fund performance in their composites if: (i) the AIMR-PPS standards requirements are met; (ii) gross and net of fee results are presented with equal prominence in a format designed to facilitate ease of comparison; and (iii) the accompanying disclosure does not identify any specific mutual fund included in the composite.

ALLOCATION OF EXPENSES

AIMR receives numerous inquiries from investment advisers that have been hired to manage a portion of an account's assets. Such multi-manager assignments are common for defined benefit plans and more recently mutual funds. In such a multi-manager account, different investment management firms manage a separate portion of the account's assets. The AIMR-PPS standards are applicable to such investment advisers who manage portions of a single account. In such cases, the fees charged may not be related at all to the investment adviser's management of assets. Such investment advisers present their composites to prospective clients for the purpose of illustrating the performance capabilities of the investment adviser.

In ICI1, the Staff recognized that certain fee arrangements, *i.e.,* those between a client and its custodian, are not subject to the control of the investment adviser and thus need not be reflected in investment adviser's performance figures. On this basis, the AIMR-PPS standards recommend that investment advisers report performance on a gross of fee basis, but only after deduction of fees and expenses related to the management of the assets by the adviser. Such fees include transaction costs and all fees or charges paid to the investment adviser or an affiliate of the investment adviser.

The AIMR-PPS Implementation Committee believes it could be misleading to require an investment adviser, which is only advising on a portion of an account's assets and is not otherwise responsible for total account operations, to report performance on a net of fee basis, after deduction of all account fees, related to the management of the assets by the adviser.

Such a presentation also would not raise concerns of the variety expressed by the Staff in the Clover and ICI1 letters.[20] It is not possible for a prospective client to invest in the particular account in reliance on something the prospective client may infer from the presentation. The presentation materials are not being shown by the investment adviser for the purpose of offering or selling the account. The purpose of the performance materials is solely to illustrate to the prospective client the capabilities of the investment adviser and enable a prospective client to make an "apples to apples" comparison of the performance history among investment advisory firms.

AIMR requests the Staff's assurance that it will not take action against AIMR members and others that claim compliance with the AIMR-PPS standards and that act as investment advisers to multimanager accounts if they present their composite performance data of the assets that the investment adviser manages, on a basis net of only those fees related to the management of the assets by the investment adviser, including transaction costs and all fees or charges paid to the investment adviser or an affiliate.

CONCLUSION

AIMR believes that the foregoing clarifications of the Staff positions will benefit investors by creating a more uniform method of presenting performance results. With the Staff's concurrence, the AIMR-PPS Implementation Committee intends to clarify the AIMR-PPS standards such that the investment advisers, when claiming compliance with the AIMR-PPS standards, are required to present the performance of similar accounts in an identical manner, as set forth above. AIMR believes that these revisions will enable investors to better conduct evaluations of investment advisers.

AIMR appreciates the attention the Staff has given to the consideration of this no-action request. The AIMR-PPS Implementation Committee welcomes the opportunity to discuss this no-action letter request with the Staff.

Sincerely yours,

/s/

Michael S. Caccese

ENDNOTES

1. AIMR is a global nonprofit membership organization consisting of investment analysts, portfolio managers and other investment decision makers. The staff views expressed in this letter are not conditioned in any way on an adviser complying with AIMR's PPS. In addition, the staff views included in this letter are in no way intended to indicate any position with respect to AIMR's PPS generally.

2. You state that a basic component of AIMR's PPS is the use of composites in investment performance presentations. You define a composite as an aggregation into a single performance presentation of portfolios or asset classes that are managed with a similar strategy or investment objective. You represent that, under the AIMR standards, all fee-paying discretionary portfolios must be included in one or more of an adviser's composites. We note that the staff has taken the position that an adviser may choose to exclude from a composite certain similarly managed accounts, so long as doing so would not cause the composite performance to be misleading. Nicholas-Applegate Mutual Funds (pub. Avail. Aug. 6, 1996).

3. The disclosure accompanying gross-of-fee performance would specifically state that the performance does not reflect the payment of investment advisory fees and other expenses that would be incurred in the management of the account.

4. The staff took the position that the presentation of gross performance data alone may be false and misleading because it could imply, or cause a potential advisory client receiving the data to infer, something about the adviser's competence or about future investment results that was not true. The Commission subsequently commenced several enforcement actions against investment advisers that advertised only gross-of-fee performance. *See In the Matter of Hazel B. Canham,* Advisers Act Rel. No. 1386 (Admin. Proc. File No. 3-8067) (Sep. 30, 1993); *In the Matter of Eric S. Emory and Renaissance Advisors, Inc.,* Advisers Act Rel. No. 1283 (Admin Proc. File No. 3-7530) (July 22, 1991); *In the Matter of Makrod Investment Associates Inc., John Thomas O'Donnell,* Advisers Act Rel. No. 1176 (Admin. Proc. File No. 3-7220) (July 3, 1989); *In the Matter of Harvest Financial Group, Inc. and Stephen S. Duklewski, Jr.,* Advisers Act Rel. No. 1155 (Admin. Proc. File no. 3-7146) (Feb. 21, 1989); *In the Matter of Managed Advisory Services, Inc. and Henry L. Chisea,* Advisers Act Rel. No. 1148 (Admin. Proc. File No. 3-7107) (Dec. 27, 1988).

5. We note that the staff has previously taken the position that an adviser's presentation of gross-of-fee performance results without net-of-fee results would not be misleading if made only in one-on-one presentations to sophisticated investors, provided that sufficient disclosures are made and the investors are given the opportunity to inquire about fees. Investment Company Institute (pub. avail. Sept. 23, 1988).

6. Rule 34b-1 under the Investment Company Act provides that sales literature for open-end funds other than money market funds, containing performance information is deemed to be misleading unless it includes, among other things, the total return calculations required under Rule 482(e) (3). *See also* Form N-1A, Item 22(b). Rule 34b-1 was adopted pursuant to Section 34(b) of the Investment Company Act, which prohibits persons from making any untrue statement of material fact in documents relating to investment companies that are required to be filed with the Commission. Advertisements and sales literature used by an open-end investment company or its underwriter must be filed, or be deemed filed, with the Commission pursuant to Section 24(b) of, or rule 24b-3 under the Investment Company Act.

7. *Cf.* Rule 135a under the Securities Act of 1933, which provides that generic advertisements that do not specifically refer by name to the securities of a particular invest-

ment company or to the investment company itself will not be deemed offers of those investment company securities if certain other conditions are met.

8. You also represent that the performance results would be accompanied by a schedule detailing the actual fees applicable to wrap fee accounts.

9. The staff addressed a similar issue in J. P. Morgan Investment Management, Inc. (pub. avail. May 7, 1996). In that letter, the staff took the position that an adviser may advertise performance reflecting the deduction of a model fee when doing so would result in performance figures that are no higher than those reflecting the deduction of actual fees.

10. For this discussion, we define a multi-manager account as a single account in which different advisory firms each manage a separate portion of the account's assets.

11. AIMR is a global non-profit membership organization with more than 60,000 members and candidates comprised of investment analysts, portfolio managers, and other investment decision makers employed by investment management firms, banks, brokerage dealers, investment company complexes, and insurance companies. AIMR's mission is to serve investors through its membership by providing global leadership in education on investment knowledge, sustaining high standards of professional conduct and administering the Chartered Financial Analyst ("CFA") designation program.

12. The AIMR-PPS standards contain both required provisions and recommended provisions. To claim compliance with the AIMR-PPS standards, a firm must comply with all of the applicable mandatory requirements of the Standards. Compliance with the AIMR-PPS standards' ethical principles often requires a firm to apply general principles of full and fair disclosure in addition to the minimum requirements and mandatory disclosures.

13. All actual, fee-paying discretionary portfolios are to be included in one or more of a firm's composites. Non-fee paying portfolios may be included in composites if such inclusion is disclosed. At least ten-year records (or since the firm's inception, if shorter) are shown in any presentation.

14. The Implementation Committee formed the Wrap Fee Subcommittee, consisting of AIMR members and staff, to address some of the issues relating to wrap fee accounts. Members of the SEC staff served as observers of the meetings of the Wrap Fee Subcommittee in which this recommendation was developed.

15. When presenting a composite for purposes of selling non-wrap fee accounts the current requirement of the AIMR-PPS standards on reporting gross or net of fees is to be followed. The AIMR-PPS standards recommend that performance be presented gross of management fees, except where this will conflict with the Staff's position on advertising performance. If the composite is presented gross of fees and includes wrap fee accounts, those wrap fee accounts must be presented either: (I) net of all fees; or (ii) net of actual transaction costs.

16. When the SEC Staff required performance results to include actual fees in *Clover Capital Management, Inc.* (October 28, 1986) (Clover), advisers that had not previously maintained records reflecting fees charged against specific accounts were unable to present historical net performance. The SEC Staff permitted the use of model fees for periods prior to May 27, 1990 in recognition of this problem.

17. The AIMR-PPS standards referred to herein apply only to mutual funds subject to the jurisdiction of the United States Federal Securities Laws.

18. The SEC has expressed a similar concern with the offer and sale of mutual funds, which is embodied in the regulations pertaining to the advertisement of mutual funds (Rule 482) and the anti-fraud rules regarding the offer and sale of mutual

funds (Rule 156). These regulations do not apply to the situation posed, however, because the performance of the mutual fund would be presented solely for comparison purposes as part of a composite presentation. Neither the individual mutual fund performance nor the identity of specific mutual funds included in the composite would be disclosed. Rather, only the composite performance of all the accounts included in the composite would be presented.

19. In ICI2, the Staff permitted the investment adviser to present performance results on a gross of fee basis in presentations in which the investment adviser met individually with an investor, and the investor had an opportunity to ask questions concerning the performance data. ICI2 also sets forth certain disclosures that are required to be made if a gross of fee presentation is used.

20. In Clover and ICI1, the Staff expressed concern that the presentation of performance results on a gross of fee basis could cause an investor to infer incorrectly something about the investment adviser's competence or about the future results of the account.

Prices Only Needed for Cash Flows to Derive True Time-Weighted Returns

To calculate true time-weighted rates of return, we only need to price portfolios on the days that cash flows occur. To prove this, we'll use the simplest rate-of-return formula, ending market value divided by beginning market value.

$$ROR = \left[\frac{EMV}{BMV} - 1\right] \cdot 100$$

Here's the scenario:

TABLE D–1

Day	Market Value
1	100
2	101
3	102
4	101
5	103
6	102
7	111
8	112
9	110
10	113

Our sample portfolio starts with a value of $100. It fluctuates during the first several days of the month. On the 7th, an inflow of $10 occurs. Let's calculate the ROR:

$$ROR = \left[\frac{101}{100} \cdot \frac{102}{101} \cdot \frac{101}{102} \cdot \frac{103}{101} \cdot \frac{102}{103} \cdot \frac{101}{102} \cdot \frac{112}{111} \cdot \frac{110}{112} \cdot \frac{113}{110} - 1 \right] \cdot 100$$

There's something interesting about this formula. Several of the factors that appear in the denominator also appear in the following numerator, and can thus be canceled:

$$ROR = \left[\frac{\cancel{101}}{100} \cdot \frac{\cancel{102}}{\cancel{101}} \cdot \frac{\cancel{101}}{\cancel{102}} \cdot \frac{\cancel{103}}{\cancel{101}} \cdot \frac{\cancel{102}}{\cancel{103}} \cdot \frac{101}{\cancel{102}} \cdot \frac{\cancel{112}}{111} \cdot \frac{\cancel{110}}{\cancel{112}} \cdot \frac{113}{\cancel{110}} - 1 \right] \cdot 100$$

Our formula now reduces to:

$$ROR = \left[\frac{101}{100} \cdot \frac{113}{111} - 1 \right] \cdot 100$$

Consequently, we find that we're measuring the return from the beginning of the period ($100) up to the point of the $10 cash flow ($101). Then, we're measuring the return from the value after the cash flow ($111) until the end of the period ($113). All the intermediate values have disappeared.

Caveat: before you discard all the daily market values during the period, it is wise to retain them until *after* the portfolios are reconciled with the custodian, in case a cash flow took place that you missed.

Mutual Fund Performance[1]

We will discuss two formulas for calculating the performance for mutual funds. The first method compares a fund's beginning and ending net asset value (NAV) in a similar way to the formula we introduced in chapter 1:

$$ROR = \left[\frac{(EMV - BMV)}{BMV} \right] * 100,$$

where

ROR = rate of return (stated as a percent)
EMV = ending market value
BMV = beginning market value

For a mutual fund, the formula is:

$$\frac{Adjusted\ NAV - Beginning\ NAV}{Beginning\ NAV} \cdot 100$$

In this calculation, we assume that any dividends are reinvested. The "Adjusted NAV" is our ending NAV, adjusted to reflect these reinvested dividends. We'll assume the following values for our example:

Beginning NAV = $9.34
Ending NAV = $9.51

Income dividend (on ex-date) = $0.0483

NAV on ex-date = $9.37

Dividends are reinvested on ex-date at the NAV on ex-date. Our first step is then to determine how many shares we can purchase for the dividend. This is found by dividing the dividend amount by the ex-date NAV:

$$\frac{Dividend\ Distribution\ Amount}{ex\text{-}date\ NAV} = \frac{.0483}{9.37} = 1.0051547$$

This value (1.0051547) is referred to as our "factor." If we were calculating the performance for a longer period, we would calculate factors for each dividend distribution date, and multiply them together.

The factor is next multiplied times our ending NAV to arrive at our adjusted NAV:

$Factor \cdot Ending\ NAV = 1.0051547 \cdot \$9.51 = 9.5590211 = Adjusted\ NAV$

We can now calculate performance for this period (using the formula we introduced at the start):

$$ROR = \frac{Adjusted\ NAV - Beginning\ NAV}{Beginning\ NAV} \cdot 100$$

$$= \frac{9.5590211 - 9.34}{9.34} \cdot 100 = \frac{0.2190211}{9.34} \cdot 100 = 0.0234497 \cdot 100 = 2.34\%$$

For our example, the fund's return is 2.34%.

We'll now discuss the formula for calculating performance for daily accrual funds. Although it may not be obvious, the formula we'll use can be thought of as an extension (albeit a nontrivial one) of the simple rate of return formula used above and first introduced in chapter 1.

The formula is:

$$P(t_a, t_b) = \frac{N_t b \left(1 + \dfrac{\sum\limits_{i=t_a}^{t_x} A_i}{N_{t_x}}\right) \cdot \left[\prod\limits_{i=t_x+1}^{t_y}\left(1 + \dfrac{D_i}{N_i}\right)\right] \cdot \left(1 + \dfrac{\sum\limits_{i=t_y+1}^{t_b} A_i}{N_{t_b}}\right) - N_{t_a}}{N_{t_a}} \cdot 100$$

where

$P(t_a, t_b)$ = total reinvestment performance (percent change) from data a to data b

A_i = per-share amount on day

D_i = per-share amount distributed (reinvested) on day I

I = day

N_{ta} = NAV on date t_a

N_{tb} = NAV on date t_b

t_x = first ex-date after t_a

t_y = last ex-date on or before t_b

N_i = NAV on day I

N_{tx} = NAV on ex-date t_x

Distributions are invested on ex-date, at the NAV on ex-date

For funds other than daily accrual funds, $A_i = 0$

For daily accrual funds, ex-date is to be understood as the accrual cycle end date (i.e., the date when the entire amount accrued in the cycle is reinvested)

This formula is more complicated because of the need to reinvest daily dividends on the appropriate distribution date(s).

We'll take this formula in pieces, starting with the numerator. Using Table E–1 as an example, we'll discuss each portion of the equation.

T A B L E   E–1

Total Reinvestment Performance Equation Example

Date	Period	Time Dividend	NAV	Equation	Factor
6/28	1 day	0.002	10.00		
6/29	1 day	0.002	10.01		
6/30	1 day	0.002	10.02	1 + [(0.002 + 0.002 + 0.002) / 10.02]	1.000598
7/31	1 month	0.002	10.10	1 + (0.062 / 10.10)	1.006138
8/31	1 month	0.002	10.20	1 + (0.062 / 10.10)	1.006078
9/1	1 day	0.002	10.21		
9/2	1 day	0.002	10.22	1 + [(0.002 + 0.002) / 10.22]	1.000391

The first factor

$$N_{t_b}\left(1 + \frac{\sum\limits_{i=t_a}^{t_x} A_i}{N_{t_x}}\right)$$

addresses the assumed reinvestment of dividends between the beginning of the performance period and the first reinvestment date. If we assume a performance period start date of June 28, with daily dividends of 0.002, and the first distribution date of June 30, the fund's NAV on June 30 is $10.02. The values for this factor become:

$$1 + \frac{0.002 + 0.002 + 0.002}{10.02} = 1.000598$$

The second factor

$$\left[\prod_{i=t_x+1}^{t_y}\left(1 + \frac{D_i}{N_i}\right)\right]$$

makes reinvestment assumptions for any full reinvestment periods occurring during the performance measurement period. Our fund continues to declare a 0.002 dividend for each calendar day. Dividends are distributed at month-end. For July, the multiplier $(1 + D_i / N_i)$ becomes:

$$1 + \frac{0.062}{10.10} = 1.006138$$

Because the reinvestment of July's dividends on July 31, redistribution-NAV of $10.10, the holding amounts to 1.006138 shares for each share held at the beginning of the previous month.

For August, this factor becomes:

$$1 + \frac{.062}{10.20} = 1.006078$$

The third factor

$$\left(1 + \frac{\sum\limits_{i=t_y+1}^{t_b} A_i}{N_{t_b}}\right)$$

addresses the reinvestment assumption for the period between the last distribution date and the end of the performance measurement period. In our example, the last distribution date is August 31 and the end of the performance measurement period is September 2. If we continue to assume daily dividends of 0.002 and an NAV of 10.22 on September 2, the factor becomes:

$$1 + \frac{(0.002 + 0.002)}{10.22} = 1.000391$$

For the performance measurement period June 28 to September 2, the total reinvestment return is:

$$\frac{[10.22 \cdot 1.000598 \cdot 1.006138 \cdot 1.006078 \cdot 1.000391) - 10.00]}{10.00} \cdot 100 = 3.555\%$$

The dividends during this period totaled $0.134 (1.34% of the initial NAV of $10.00). The fund's NAV increased from $10.00 to $10.22 in the period—a 2.2% gain. Add the aggregate dividend return to the NAV's percentage change, and the total return is 1.34% + 2.2% = 3.54% The difference between this value and the calculated value (3.555%) is caused by the daily compounding at each distribution date. This compounding equates with an investor who accumulates additional shares every reinvestment date as accrued dividends are reinvested. These equations are assumed to be adjusted for any splits and capital gain distributions.

The total return performance results describe the performance of the investment portfolio and not necessarily the actual experience an investor might have. This approach does not assume that shares were purchased at the beginning of the period with a sales charge applied, or that shares were sold at the end of the period with a redemption fee or deferred sales charge applied.

ENDNOTE

1. Most of the information (including the examples) contained in this appendix was provided by Tom Cotterell of Lipper Analytical Services.

Present Value Tables

Chapter 1 discussed how, before computers, present value tables were used to determine the present value of future cash flows, to assist in investment decisions. We'll use Table F–1 (an abbreviated example of a present value table) to demonstrate how this is done.

TABLE   F–1

Present Value Table

Period (years)	1%	2%	3%	4%	5%	10%
1	0.990	0.980	0.971	0.962	0.952	0.909
2	0.980	0.961	0.943	0.925	0.907	0.826
3	0.971	0.942	0.915	0.889	0.864	0.751
4	0.961	0.924	0.888	0.855	0.823	0.683
5	0.951	0.906	0.863	0.822	0.784	0.621
6	0.942	0.888	0.837	0.790	0.746	0.564
7	0.933	0.871	0.813	0.760	0.711	0.513
8	0.923	0.853	0.789	0.731	0.677	0.467
9	0.914	0.837	0.766	0.703	0.645	0.424
10	0.905	0.820	0.744	0.676	0.614	0.386

Table F–1 only shows rates of 1% to 5% and 10% and for 1-10 years. Larger tables, covering more interest rates and years, are available, but this will suffice for our demonstration.

In chapter 1, we determined (through the use of a present value formula) that at a 10% annual rate of return, a $1,000 investment will become $1,611 in 5 years. Or, stated simply, $1,000 is the *present value* of $1,611 in 5 years at 10%. We'll show how this can be determined via the present value table.

Table F–1 shows the present value of $1 invested at various interest rates over various periods of time. For example, the intersection of 5 years and 5% shows the figure 0.784. This means that having 78.4 cents today equals $1 in 5 years, if our expected annual rate of return is 5%. We can validate this by simply multiplying 0.784 by 1.05 five times (the equivalent of compounding a 5% interest rate for 5 years). Doing this, we obtain a value of 1.0006, or 1 dollar (the .0006 is due to rounding).

Let's get back to our example from chapter 1. Here, we want to get the value from Table F–1 for the period of 5 years for a rate of 10%. This value is 0.621. Since this table is for an investment of $1, we must multiply this value times $1,611 to get the equivalent present value. Doing this, we get 1000.431, or $1000 (the .431 is due to rounding).

Glossary

Accruals (also, accrued income, income accruals): Fixed-income securities (bonds) and other securities that pay income on a regular basis (e.g., semiannually). The income amount accumulates over time, up to the date the interest payment is actually made. This accumulation is referred to as an *accrual*. The value of the security includes its market price and any income accumulation. Should the owner of a security decide to sell it, he is entitled to receive the amount that has been accrued up to the settlement date of the trade.

Attribution: The act of *attributing* an event to its underlying cause or causes, that is, determining what action(s) contributed to an event. Performance attribution is a way of determining what contributed to the resulting rate of return.

Bank Administration Institute (BAI): This banking organization developed detailed performance presentation standards in 1968 that resulted in a shift away from *dollar-weighted* rates of return to *time-weighted* rates of return. The "BAI Standards" were adopted by many banks and other investment organizations.

Capitalization: We often refer to stocks as being *small cap, mid cap,* or *large cap.* The "cap" refers to capitalization. This is also the value of the company, as perceived by the marketplace, at any given time. It's calculated by multiplying the stock's current market price by the number of shares outstanding. This, in essence, is what the market says the company is worth.

Cash Allocation: This is the process of dividing cash between the various asset classes (e.g., fixed-income, equities, real estate). The allocation process shouldn't be arbitrary, but should reflect the cash that is being *earmarked* for investment in the asset to which it's being allocated. Chapter 3 discusses various methods of allocating cash.

Composite: A collection of one or more portfolios (or portions of portfolios), grouped together because they have similar investment styles, objectives, and characteristics. Composites are typically created to comply with the AIMR-PPS and to provide a reasonable way for prospective clients to evaluate a firm's history in investing to meet their individual objectives.

Compounding: The arithmetic process of determining the final value of an asset when income is realized over time. Compounding can occur at discrete time periods (e.g., monthly, quarterly, semiannually) or continuously (continuous compounding). In calculating rates of return, compounding reflects subsequent income being realized on prior period income.

Correlation: A statistical tool to help analyze the *closeness* between two or more variables. This statistic can range from +1 to 1. A value of +1 suggests perfect correlation, meaning the variables move in the same direction and by the same magnitude 100% of the time. A value of 1 suggests perfect negative correlation (like two politicians who never agree). These variables would move in opposite directions, by the same relative magnitude.

Dollar-Weighted Rate of Return: A method of deriving a rate of return that can be influenced by cash flows that take place in the account. An example of a formula that derives a dollar-weighted return is the internal rate of return (IRR). Contrast with *time-weighted rates of return.*

Ex-Date: The date the price of a security will no longer reflect the presence of a pending dividend payment. Purchasers of a stock on or after ex-date of a company that has announced a dividend payment won't be entitled to the payment, so the stock price doesn't reflect the dividend. "Ex-" means "without"; in this case, without the dividend.

Hedging: This term probably comes from the expression, to *hedge* one's bet. Basically, it's a way to attempt to reduce your risk or exposure by taking some other action. A decision to purchase foreign securities for a U.S. investor introduces a new risk— currency exposure. The decision to buy a security from another country is probably being made because that market is felt to be an attractive one, or that particular company is. Currency rates can fluctuate, which can result in a loss in any appreciation that might occur in the security that's purchased. To offset this risk, managers may purchase future contracts in the currency of the country they're investing in. For example, let's say a Japanese security costs 10 million yen. Eventually, the security will be sold and the yen converted back to dollars. If in the intervening period, the dollar strengthens against the yen, less dollars would be purchased when converting. To reduce this exposure, the manager could purchase a future contract to sell ten million yen at a given exchange rate. This way, regardless of what the currency markets do, the manager knows she can obtain dollars at a known rate once the security is sold. A foreign investment that doesn't have such hedging applied is referred to as an *unhedged* position.

Internal Rate of Return (IRR): The dollar-weighted rate of return on an investment. The IRR is calculated by finding the discount rate that equates the present value of future cash flows to the cost (or dividend rate) of the investment. The IRR is the rate of return that equates the present value of the expected future receipts to the cost of the investment outlay. The IRR method is also referred to as the discounted cash flow (DCF) method, the time-adjusted return method, or the investor's method.

Investment Counsel Association of America (ICAA): An independent organization that represents the interests of independent investment counseling firms. Member firms are not affiliated with other entities, such as insurance companies, banks, or brokerage firms. The ICAA is responsible for the development of a set of performance standards in 1971 that permitted its members and others to report time-weighted rates of return in a way that didn't require the use of a computer.

Net Present Value (NPV): A method of ranking investment proposals by determining the future value of an investment given a defined dividend or interest rate, or by finding the present value if the future value is known, given the rate. The NPV is the basis for the internal rate of return formula.

No-Action Letter: This is a letter the SEC provides in which they state they will not take action against a firm if the firm behaves in a certain manner. The SEC has established certain regulations. At times, a firm will want an exception to a regulation. They explain their situation to the SEC in writing, and if the SEC concurs, the SEC will write a *no-action* letter that gives the conditions under which they will not recommend enforcement action (i.e., no action).

Price/Earnings Ratio: Also called P/E, this ratio is one way to assess the market's view of a stock. Higher-P/E stocks generally reflect situations where investors anticipate an increase in earnings or growth. Lower-P/E stocks reflect the opposite. For example, a stock that is priced at 40 times earnings (e.g., a price of $80 with earnings of $2) is priced higher relative to one that has a P/E of 20 (a $40 stock with $2 earnings).

Rate of Return (ROI): A percentage that reflects the appreciation (or depreciation) in the value of an account, portfolio, subportfolio, or other asset. See *time-weighted rates of return* and *dollar-weighted rates of return*.

Reconciliation: The accounting system that a money manager uses to keep track of his client portfolios is normally not "official." In most cases, the *official books and records* of the account are maintained by the client's custodian. Money managers typically *reconcile* their books with the custodian on a monthly basis, to determine if there exist any out-of-balance situations. This is analogous to individuals' checking accounts. Their checkbook reflects what *they* believe their balance to be. However, the *official books and records* are those of the bank. Like money managers, individuals should reconcile their checkbook with their bank statement periodically to make sure they have properly accounted for everything. Being the *official books and records* doesn't mean the custodian is always right. On occasion, they may make an error. The reconciliation is a way of identifying problems so they can be brought to the proper party for correction.

Record Date: The date on which an entity (e.g., an individual, a pension plan) must be registered as a shareholder of a company in order to receive a declared dividend.

R^2, or R-squared: This statistic reflects the percentage of a portfolio's movements that can be explained by movements in its benchmark. A high R-squared represents a strong relationship between the portfolio and its benchmark; a low R-squared represents a weak relationship. Some style analysis techniques use R-squared as a way to find the benchmark that best relates to the portfolio.

Time-Weighted Rates of Return: A return method that eliminates the impact of cash flows on the resulting performance calculations. Since money managers typically don't have responsibility for cash flows, their returns shouldn't be influenced by these flows. A formula that provides time-weighted rates of return eliminates this effect. Contrast with *dollar-weighted rates of return.*

Total Return: The return on an account that reflects both capital appreciation and income. Alternatively, one could measure the return on principal (excluding income) or income only. The returns discussed in this book are total returns.

Unhedged: A security position or investment that isn't *hedged.* See *hedging.*

Selected References

Antilla, Susan. "This Money Manager Can't Count." *The New York Times* (June 20, 1993), p. 15.

Balzer, Leslie A. "Measuring Investment Risk: A Review." *The Journal of Investing* (Fall 1995).

Brinson, Gary P., L. Randolph Hood, and Gilbert L. Beebower. "Determinants of Portfolio Performance." *Financial Analysts Journal*, vol. 51, no. 1 (January/February 1995), pp. 133–48.

Christopherson, Jon A., and C. Nola Williams. "Equity Style: What It Is and Why It Matters," in *The Handbook of Equity Style Management*, T. Daniel Coggin and Frank J. Fabozzi, eds. (New Hope, Pa.: Frank J. Fabozzi Associates, 1995).

Christopherson, Jon A., and Dennis J. Trittin. "Equity Style Classification System," in *The Handbook of Equity Style Management*, T. Daniel Coggin and Frank J. Fabozzi, eds. (New Hope, Pa.: Frank J. Fabozzi Associates, 1995).

Dietz, P. O. *Pension Funds: Measuring Investment Performance* (New York: The Free Press, 1966).

Farrell, James L., Jr. *Guide to Portfolio Management* (New York: McGraw-Hill Book Company, 1976).

Foss, Gregory W. "Quantifying Risk in the Corporate Bond Markets." *Financial Analysts Journal*, vol. 51, no. 2 (March/April 1995), pp. 29–41.

Hardy, Steve. "Return-Based Style Analysis," in *The Handbook of Equity Style Management*, T. Daniel Coggin and Frank J. Fabozzi, eds. (New Hope, Pa.: Frank J. Fabozzi Associates, 1995).

Hardy, Steve. "Excess Return for Index Fund ..." *Pensions & Investments* (January 6, 1997) p. 10.

Jorion, Philippe. "Risk^2 Measuring the Risk in Value at Risk." *Financial Analysts Journal*, vol 52, no. 6 (November/December 1996), pp. 47–56.

Kaplan, Paul D. "Measuring Risk: The Unseen Enemy," in *The Journal of Performance Measurement*, Paul D. Kaplan, ed., vol. 1, no. 2 (1996).

Kaplan, Paul D., and Marius Daugirdas. "Traditional vs. New Forms of Risk Measure." *Pensions & Investments* (November 25, 1996), p. 12.

Karnosky, Denis S., and Brian D. Singer. *Global Asset Management and Performance Attribution*. The Research Foundation of The Institute of Chartered Financial Analysts, 1994.

Kirschman, Jeannette, and Peter O. Dietz. "Evaluating Portfolio Performance," in *Managing Investment Portfolios*, John L. Maginn & Donald L. Tuttle, eds. (Boston: The Institute of Chartered Financial Analysts, 1983).

Lerit, Steven J. "Measuring the Impact of Cash Flows and Market Volatility on Investment Performance Results." *The Journal of Performance Measurement* (Winter 1996).

McConnell, Nancy Belliveau. "Can Phony Performance Numbers Be Policed?" *Institutional Investor* (June 1989), pp. 91–104.

Posey, Ann. "How to Evaluate Manager Style and Skill." *Pension Management* (February 1996).

Riddles, Neil. "Comparing Equity Indexes." *IIR Performance Measurement Conference* (June 5, 1996).

Sharpe, William F. "Determining a Fund's Effective Asset Mix." *Investment Management Review* (November/December 1988), pp. 59–69.

Sharpe, William F. "Asset Allocation: Management Style and Performance Attribution," *The Journal of Portfolio Management* (Winter 1992), pp. 7–19.

Sharpe, William F. "The Sharpe Ratio." *The Journal of Portfolio Management* (Fall 1994), pp. 49–58.

Sieff, John A. "Measuring Investment Performance: The Unit Approach." *Financial Analysts Journal* (July/August 1966), pp. 93–99.

Singer, Brian D. "Evaluation of Portfolio Performance: Attribution Analysis." *The Journal of Performance Measurement* (Winter 1996), pp. 45–55.

Sortino, Frank A., and Hal J. Forssey. "Style Risk: Resolving the Time Sensitivity Problem." *The Journal of Performance Measurement*, (Fall 1996).

Spurr, William A., and Charles P. Bonini. *Statistical Analysis for Business Decisions* (Homewood, Ill.: Richard D. Irwin, Inc., 1973).

Surz, Ronald J. "Portfolio Opportunity Distributions: An Innovation in Performance Evaluation." The Journal of Investing (Summer 1994).

———. "Portfolio Opportunity Distributions: A Solution to the Problems With Benchmarks and Peer Groups." *The Journal of Performance Measurement* (Winter 1996).

———. "Solving the Performance Puzzle." *Pension Management* (May 1996).

Ward, Judy. "Risk Matters: Using Downside Risk Analysis to Set Plan Options and Help Participants Make Choices." *Plan Sponsor* (September 1996), pp. 57–58.

Weston, J. Fred, and Eugene F. Brigham. *Essentials of Managerial Finance* (Hinsdale, Ill.: The Dryden Press, 1974).

White, James A. "How a Money Manager Can Pull a Rabbit Out of a Hat." *The Wall Street Journal* (March 16, 1989).

Williams, Arthur. "Measurement and Comparison of Investment Performance." *The Financial Analyst's Handbook,* 2d ed., Sumner N. Levine, ed. (Homewood, Ill: Dow Jones-Irwin, 1988).

"A 'Can't Miss' Mutual-Fund Machine Sputters." *The Wall Street Journal* (November 22, 1996), p. C1.

"An Index: A Bogey or Bogus? *Ryan Labs Review* (First Quarter 1994), pp. 1–2.

"Answers to Common Questions About AIMR's Performance Presentation Standards." Association for Investment Management and Research, 1992.

Measuring the Investment of Pension Funds (Park Ridge, Ill.: Bank Administration Institute [BAI], 1968).

Morningstar Mutual Funds User's Guide (Chicago: Morningstar, 1996).

"New Russell Software Scrutinizes Portfolio Style." *Global Investment Technology* (December 9, 1996), pp. 10–11.

Performance Measurement Techniques [date unknown], Sanford C. Bernstein & Co., Inc.

Performance Measurement: Setting the Standards, Interpreting the Numbers. The Institute of Chartered Financial Analysts and the Financial Analysts Federation, 1989.

Performance Measurement Surveys—Summary Results June 1995. The Spaulding Group, 1995.

Performance Reporting for Investment Managers: Applying the AIMR Performance Presentation Standards. Association for Investment Management and Research, 1991.

Performance Presentation Standards 1993. Association for Investment Management and Research, 1993.

Report of the Performance Presentation Standards Implementation Committee. Association for Investment Management and Research, 1991.

"Risk Management Systems: Exposure Management Is Top Priority as Firms Search for Systems Solutions." *Global Investment Technology* (January 24, 1994).

Second Edition AIMR Performance Presentation Standards Handbook 1997. Association for Investment Management and Research, 1996.

Study of the Investment Performance of ERISA Plans. Berkowitz, Logue & Associates, July 21, 1986.

"Style Analysis." *Ryan Labs Review,* Special Edition (Ryan Labs, 1996).

The Standards of Measurement and Use for Investment Performance Data. Investment Council Association of America, Inc., 1971.

Index